Modern England, 1901—1970

CONFERENCE ON BRITISH STUDIES
BIBLIOGRAPHICAL HANDBOOKS

Editor: J. JEAN HECHT

Consultant Editor: G.R. ELTON

Modern England
1901-1970

ALFRED F. HAVIGHURST
Amherst College ₁ᵤ

CAMBRIDGE UNIVERSITY PRESS
CAMBRIDGE
LONDON · NEW YORK · MELBOURNE
for the Conference on British Studies

Published by the Syndics of the Cambridge University Press
The Pitt Building, Trumpington Street, Cambridge CB2 1RP
Bentley House, 200 Euston Road, London NW1 2DB
32 East 57th Street, New York, NY 10022, USA
296 Beaconsfield Parade, Middle Park, Melbourne 3206, Australia

First published 1976

Printed in Great Britain
at the University Printing House, Cambridge
(Euan Phillips, University Printer)

Library of Congress Cataloguing in Publication Data

Havighurst, Alfred F.

Modern England, 1901—1970.

(Conference on British Studies bibliographical handbooks)

Includes index.

1. Great Britain — Civilization — 20th century — Bibliography. 2. Great Britain —
History — 20th century — Bibliography. I. Title. II. Series: Conference on British
Studies. Bibliographical handbooks.
Z2020.H38   [DA566.4]   016.941   75-23844
ISBN 0 521 20941 2

CONTENTS

PREFACE

In purpose this volume follows the course set by the other volumes in this series already published. *Modern England, 1901–1970* is a bibliographical handbook designed as a ready book of reference for the scholar, for the teacher, for the student, and for the general reader interested in exploring this period in some depth. It is a bibliography of published material, including primary sources (official records and documents, memoirs, diaries, letters, etc.) as well as secondary (monographs, biographies and articles). It does not provide detailed direction to unpublished manuscripts, to archives, or to microfilm, though it does supply general guides to such classifications.

The selection of books and articles rests upon a comprehensive search of historical literature published before 1 January 1974. However, some of the more important titles which appeared early in 1974 have been also included. The arbitrary editorial limit of about 2500 items, while precluding any attempt at completeness, is sufficiently large to provide a representation of English life and society in the twentieth century which is both broad and deep. Of the major aspects of English life, only literature *per se* is excluded; however, a few items on literary history and on the lives of significant writers are included. The primary basis of selection has been that of scholarly usefulness to student, teacher and researcher, but some competent books of general interest, lacking documentation, are listed, particularly if nothing else in the area is available. A few titles are included not so much because they are significant in themselves as because they represent areas in which more adequate treatment is needed.

Each volume in this series has had its special problems. In the present instance perhaps the chief difficulty has been that of distinguishing the historical past from the contemporary present. As A.J.P. Taylor puts it, history becomes 'thicker' as we approach the present. There is more of it — more historical evidence and more writing about that evidence. But is it all 'history'? Is not much of it current events, or journalism, or social commentary? Such questions arise repeatedly, for history not only gets 'thicker', it gets less distinct. Al illuminating discussion of this matter will be found in Chapter 1, 'Since 1914: Recent or Contemporary?' of (40) of this volume.

A practical difficulty is added by the rapidly changing character of the materials with which the historian of twentieth-century Britain works. As late as 1965 scholars were barred from using documents of the Foreign Office and other government departments later than 1914. But in 1967 the Public Records Statute replaced the fifty-year rule with the thirty-year rule. At once became available a flood of material for the period between the wars. A similar letting down of bars at the British Museum and other repositories followed, and private individuals possessing important manuscript collections now readily made them available. Much primary material, difficult of access not many years ago, is now on microfilm. In consequence, in the past fifteen years there has been a flood of monographs and articles on all aspects of twentieth-century Britain. A bibliography assembled in 1974 is quite different from one which would have been put together only ten or twelve years ago.

To cope in some degree with the mass of material which may be called historical literature and to include in this volume as much as possible of that which seems useful and relevant I have somewhat modified previous practice in this series. In the first place I have tried to avoid unnecessary overlapping from the previous volume in this series: Josef L. Altholz, *Victorian England, 1837–1901* (1970). It has been common practice for historians writing on the nineteenth century, particularly those in economic or diplomatic history, to carry their period over to 1914 as a convenient terminal date. I have excluded a considerable number of those items which are largely concerned with Victorian England; I *have* included those which emphasize the twentieth century. New titles relating to both periods as well as revisions since the appearance of the Altholz volume will be found in the present volume. But for complete bibliographical information on the period 1901–14 both handbooks should be consulted.

A new category, 'Urban History' has been introduced in recognition of the emergence in our day of that area as a distinct field of study. Also this permits more exactness in locating certain items which otherwise might easily fall into two or more categories. The attention of the reader particularly interested in Naval and Military History is at once directed to the note introducing that section.

Empire and Commonwealth receive, relatively, somewhat more attention than in the volume on Victorian England, since their history has more directly affected the fortunes of Britain in the twentieth century. But items on the internal history of particular colonies or dominions are excluded. Fairly wide coverage is accorded Ireland until the formation of the Irish Free State in 1922. For Scotland, items of general interest, especially those associating it with England, will be found. As in the Altholz handbook, legal history is under Constitutional and Administrative History; journalism and political and economic thought under Intellectual History. The history of education — an extensive field — is divided: at the lower levels it will be found under Social History; higher education and adult education with Intellectual History. Some titles, of necessity, have been assigned to particular categories rather arbitrarily. Cross-references at the beginning of certain sections should assist in locating relevant material.

The annotations represent my own evaluations though often influenced by the judgement of others. In particular I have sought to compensate for the limitations of certain titles and to indicate more clearly their contents. Cross-references will be found annexed to certain items; the reader is urged to use these references to bring together related material.

In the preparation of this handbook I have incurred many obligations.
Dr J. Jean Hecht, the Series Editor, carefully reviewed the manuscript. The
Consultant Editor, Professor G.R. Elton, has been generous with encourage-
ment and counsel; he sustained me when my enthusiasm flagged. Professors
J.B. Connacher and T.O. Lloyd of the University of Toronto found time
during a busy academic year for a critical examination of the typescript;
their informed comments were much appreciated. I am grateful to them
all. This handbook was prepared largely from the holdings of the following
libraries: Amherst College, Smith College, University of Massachusetts,
Harvard University, and the Episcopal Theological School, Cambridge,
Mass. To the members of their staffs I wish to express my deep thanks for
the countless ways in which they facilitated my task.

Amherst, Massachusetts
March, 1975   ALFRED F. HAVIGHURST

ABBREVIATIONS

AHR	*American Historical Review*
BH	*Business History*
BIHR	*Bulletin of the Institute of Historical Research*
BJES	*British Journal of Educational Studies*
BJS	*British Journal of Sociology*
EcHR	*Economic History Review*
EHR	*English Historical Review*
EJ	*Economic Journal*
Ess. Lab. Hist.	*Essays in Labour History 1886–1923*, ed. Asa Briggs and John Saville, 1971.
GJ	*Geographical Journal*
Hist. J.	*Historical Journal*
IHS	*Irish Historical Studies*
IRSH	*International Review of Social History*
JBS	*Journal of British Studies*
JCH	*Journal of Contemporary History*
JEcH	*Journal of Economic History*
JHI	*Journal of the History of Ideas*
JMH	*Journal of Modern History*
JTH	*Journal of Transport History*
NCMH	*The New Cambridge Modern History*, ed. G.N. Clark *et al.* Vol. XII (2nd ed.), *The Shifting Balance of World Forces 1898–1945*, ed. C.L. Mowat (Cambridge, 1968).
PA	*Public Administration*
PP	*Past and Present*
PS	*Political Studies*
SHR	*Scottish Historical Review*
TRHS	*Transactions of the Royal Historical Society*
YBESR	*Yorkshire Bulletin of Economic and Social Research*

EXPLANATORY NOTES

1. In matters of editorial style I have generally followed the practice in Josef L. Altholz, *Victorian England, 1837–1901* (1970), of this series.

2. When no place of publication is indicated for a book, its place of publication is London. When a book appeared in two or more places the place of publication of the copy examined by the compiler is given.

3. If a work appeared under one title in the United Kingdom and under another in the United States, both titles are normally provided.

4. Printed sources are generally listed under the names of the authors when they were responsible for original publication; otherwise under the name of the editor.

I. BIBLIOGRAPHIES

1   Albion, Robert Greenhalgh. *Naval and maritime history; an annotated bibliography*. 4th ed., Mystic, Conn., 1972. Useful sections on Great Britain.

2   Allen, Victor L. *International bibliography of trade unionism*. 1968.

3   *American Historical Review*. 'Other recent publications', *AHR*, XLII– (1936–). Title varies; since 1970, 'Recently published articles'. The section on 'Great Britain, Commonwealth and Ireland', while incomplete, is useful.

4   *Annual bibliography of the history of British art*. 1936–. Begins with 1934 publications. In 1938 title changes to *Bibliography of British art*.

5   *Annual bulletin of historical literature*. 1912–. Published by the Historical Association. Begins with publications of 1911; includes a section on 'Contemporary History', later 'The Twentieth Century'. Though a time-lag, this is an essential reference.

6   *A bibliography of the history of Wales*. 2nd ed., Cardiff, 1962.

7   Brophy, Jacqueline. 'Bibliography of British labor and radical journals, 1880–1914'. *Labor History*, III (Winter 1962), 103–26.

8   *British national bibliography, 1950–*. 1951–. Weekly list of books published in Great Britain brought together in annual volumes; cumulative indexes for 1950–70.

9   Bulkley, Mildred E. *Bibliographical survey of contemporary sources for the economic and social history of the war*. Oxford, 1922. On World War I.

10   Carty, James. *Bibliography of Irish history, 1912–1921*. Dublin, 1936. See also his *Bibliography of Irish history, 1870–1911*. Dublin, 1940.

11   Chrimes, Stanley B. and Ivan A. Roots (eds.). *English constitutional history: a select bibliography* (Helps for Students of History, no. 58). 1958.

12   Crombie, Alistair C. and M.A. Hoskin (eds.). *History of science: an annual review of literature, research and teaching*. Cambridge, 1962–. Editorship and subtitle change with vol. XI (1973).

13   *Economic History Review*. 'List of publications on the economic history of Great Britain and Ireland', *EcHR*, I– (1927–). Issued annually; title varies. Thorough coverage of documents, monographs and articles.

14   Elton, Geoffrey R. *Modern historians on British history, 1485–1945; a critical bibliography, 1945–1969*. Ithaca, N.Y., 1970. Substantial section on twentieth century.

15   Emmison, Frederick G. (ed.). *English local history handlist* (Helps for Students of History, no. 69). 4th ed., 1969.

16   *English Historical Review*. 'Notices of periodicals and occasional publications', *EHR*, XXXIX– (1924–). Issued annually in July; title varies; selective.

17   Falls, Cyril B. *War books: a critical guide*. 1930. Useful for publications of the 1920s.

18   Ferguson, Eugene S. (ed.). *Bibliography of the history of technology*. Cambridge, Mass., 1968. 'A reasonably comprehensive introduction to primary and secondary sources.' For more recent publications, see (23).

19   Filby, P. William. *American and British genealogy and heraldry: a selected list of books*. Chicago, 1970.

20   Frow, Ruth and Edmund and Michael Katanka. *The history of British trade unions: a select bibliography*. 1969. Published by the Historical Association.

21   Frewer, Louis B. (ed.). *Bibliography of historical writings published in Britain and the Empire, 1940–1945*. Oxford, 1947.

22   Gaskell, Philip. *A new introduction to bibliography*. Oxford, 1972. Successor to Ronald B. McKerrow, *An introduction to bibliography for literary students*. 1927.

23   Goodwin, Jack (ed.). 'Current bibliography in the history of technology', *Technology and Culture*, V– (1964–). This first list is for 1962; annual since then. Is now the definitive international current bibliography.

24   Gulick, Charles A. and Roy A. Ockert and Raymond J. Wallace (eds.).

1

History and theories of working-class movements: a select bibliography. Berkeley, Cal., 1955.
25 Hancock, Philip D. *A bibliography of works relating to Scotland 1916—1950.* Edinburgh, 1959—60, 2 vols.
26 Higham, Robin D.S. (ed.). *A guide to the sources of British military history.* 1972. The most complete guide for the twentieth century.
27 'Histories of the First and Second World Wars' (H.M.S.O., Sectional List no. 60). 1967. For commentary see Higham. 'The history of the Second World War, British Official Series', *The Library Quarterly*, XXXIV (July 1964), 240—8.
28 Howe, George F. *et al.* (eds.). *The American Historical Association's guide to historical literature.* New York, 1961. Selective on twentieth century. Replaces George Matthew Dutcher *et al.* (eds.), *Guide to historical literature.* (New York, 1931).
29 *International bibliography of historical sciences.* Paris, 1930—. Begins with works published in 1926. Volume for 1968—9 was published in 1971.
30 *Labour Party bibliography.* 1967. Comprehensive on printed materials, most of which are available at Transport House.
31 Kellaway, William (ed.). *Bibliography of historical works issued in the United Kingdom, 1957—60.* 1962.
32 —— *Bibliography of historical works issued in the United Kingdom, 1961—65.* 1967.
33 —— *Bibliography of historical works issued in the United Kingdom, 1966—70.* 1972.
34 Lancaster, Joan C. (ed.). *Bibliography of historical works issued in the United Kingdom, 1946—1956.* 1957.
35 Maehl, William H. Jr., ' "Jerusalem deferred": recent writing in the history of the British labor movement', *JMH*, XLI (Sept. 1969), 335—67. Essential for any serious investigation. Cites earlier review articles on labour movement by Charles Loch Mowat.
36 Martin, Geoffrey H. and Sylvia McIntyre. *A bibliography of British and Irish municipal history*, I, *general works.* Leicester, 1972.
37 Matthews, William (ed.). *British autobiographies: an annotated bibliography of British autobiographies published or written before 1951.* Berkeley, Cal., 1955.
38 —— *British diaries: an annotated bibliography of British diaries written between 1442 and 1942.* Berkeley, Cal., 1950.
39 Mowat, Charles Loch. *British history since 1926: a select bibliography* (Helps for Students of History, no. 61). 1960.
40 —— *Great Britain since 1914* (The Sources of History: studies in the Uses of Historical Evidence). Ithaca, N.Y., 1971. Useful commentary on the nature and value of available historical evidence.
41 Mullins, Edward L.C. *Guide to the historical and archaeological publications of societies in England and Wales 1901—1933.* 1968. Indexes titles and authors.
42 Ottley, George (ed.). *A bibliography of British railway history.* 1965.
43 Rider, Kenneth J. *History of science and technology: a select bibliography for students.* 2nd ed., 1970. Published by the Library Association. Indispensable.
44 Thompson, Theodore R. (ed.). *A catalog of British family histories.* 2nd ed., 1935.
45 Whitrow, Magda (ed.). *ISIS cumulative bibliography: a bibliography of the history of science formed from ISIS critical bibliographies 1—90, 1913—65.* 1971, 2 vols. Thereafter published annually; indispensable for specialists.
46 Winkler, Henry R. 'Some recent writings on twentieth-century Britain', in Elizabeth C. Furber (ed.). *Changing views on British history: essays on historical writing since 1939.* Cambridge, Mass., 1966, pp. 289—319.
47 Winks, Robin W. (ed.). *The historiography of the British Empire—Commonwealth: trends, interpretations, and resources.* Durham, N.C., 1966.

48 Woods, Frederick (ed.). *A bibliography of the works of Sir Winston Churchill*. 2nd ed., Toronto, 1969.
49 *Writings on British history, 1901—1933*. 1968—70, 5 vols.
50 *Writings on British history, 1934—1945*. ed.   Alexander Taylor Milne. 1937—60, 8 vols.
51 *Writings on British history, 1946—1948*. ed. Donald James Munro. 1973. Exhaustive on British history before 1914 and selective thereafter.

II. CATALOGUES, GUIDES, AND HANDBOOKS

52 Abraham, Louis A. and Stephen C. Hawtrey, *A parliamentary dictionary*. 1956.
53 *Abstract of labour statistics*. 1894—1937. Periodic reports of the Labour Department of the Board of Trade and later of the Ministry of Labour. Title varies.
54 *The annual register 1900—*. 1901—. An annual narrative of events, largely from newspaper sources, which appears within six months after the year concerned.
55 *Bartholomew's reference atlas of greater London*. 13th ed. Edinburgh, 1968. Has extraordinary detail.
56 Bellamy, Joyce M. and John Saville (eds.). *Dictionary of labour biography*, I–II. 1970, 1974. Other volumes to follow. Each volume is self-contained, A to Z.
57 Bickmore, David P. and M.A. Shaw. *The atlas of Great Britain and Northern Ireland*. Oxford, 1963. Superb.
58 Boehm, Eric H. and Adolphus Lalit. *Historical periodicals*. Santa Barbara, Cal., 1961. Has section on Great Britain.
59 Bond, Maurice F. *Guide to the records of parliament*. 1971. Carries through session of 1969—70.
60 *Britain, 1948/9, an official handbook*, 1948—. Annual; the 23rd handbook appeared in 1972. Prepared by the Central Office of Information; the best brief reference book.
61 *British labour statistics yearbook 1969—*. H.M.S.O., 1971—. Latest volume, for 1971, was published in 1973. This series follows *British labour statistics: historical abstracts*, 1886—1968 (1971) and together form a useful and convenient reference.
62 British Museum. *Catalogue of additions to the manuscripts in the British Museum 1900—*. 1907—. Periodic volumes.
63 —— *The catalogues of the manuscript collections*, ed. T.C. Skeat. Rev. ed., 1962.
64 —— *General catalogue of printed books ... to 1955*. Photolithographic edition. 1965—6, 263 vols. *Ten year supplement 1956—1965*. 1968, 50 vols. *Five year supplement 1966—70*. 1971—2, 26 vols.
65 —— *Subject index of the modern works added ... in the years 1901—1905*. 1906. Quinquennially, thereafter; title varies. Latest is for 1956—60. 1965—6, 6 vols.
66 Butler, David and Jennie Freeman. *British political facts 1900—1967*. 2nd ed., 1968. Includes economic data.
67 *Catalogue of government publications, 1956—*. H.M.S.O., 1927—. Title varies. The latest volume is for publications in 1972 (1973). Continues *Consolidated list of government publications* (1937—). Both assemble *Government publications: monthly list, 1936—*. H.M.S.O., 1937.
68 *Census reports of Great Britain, 1901—1931* (Guides to Official Sources, no. 2). H.M.S.O., 1951. For subsequent censuses (there was none in 1941) consult *Census of England and Wales, preliminary report* and other reports in (67).
69 Cheney, Christopher R. *Handbook of dates for students of English history* (Royal Historical Society Guides and Handbooks, no. 4). 1945.

70   C[okayne], G[eorge] E. *The complete peerage of England, Scotland, Ireland,
     Great Britain and the United Kingdom, extant, extinct, or dormant*, rev.
     by Vicary Gibbs. New ed., 1910—59, 13 vols in 14. Title and editors vary.
     Vol. 13, ed. H.A. Doubleday and Lord Howard de Walden, is *Peers
     created 1901—1938*. 1940. This is the best guide to the peerage.

71   Craig, Frederick W.S. (ed.). *British parliamentary results 1918—1949*.
     Glasgow, 1969.

72   —— *British parliamentary election results 1950—1970*. Chichester, 1971.

73   —— *British parliamentary statistics, 1918—1968*. 1968. See also Craig's
     Boundaries of parliamentary constituencies 1885—1972. 1972.

74   *Crockford's clerical directory for 1860—*. 1860—. Annual or semi-annual;
     latest issue is for 1971—2 (1973); 'a statistical book of reference'.

75   Crone, John S. (ed.). *A concise dictionary of Irish biography*. Rev. ed.,
     Dublin, 1937.

76   *The dictionary of national biography. Second supplement*. 1912, 3 vols. Bi-
     ographies of 'noteworthy persons' who died 1901—11. *Supplement,
     1912—1921*. 1927. *Supplement, 1922—1930*. 1937. *Supplement, 1931—
     1940*. 1949. *Supplement, 1941—50*. 1959. *Supplement, 1951—60*. 1971.
     An epitomé is in *The concise dictionary: pt. II, 1901—1950*. 1961.

77   Di Roma, Edward and Joseph A. Rosenthal. *A numerical finding list of
     British command papers, published 1833—1961/62*. New York, 1967.

78   [Dod, Charles Roger Phipps]. *Dod's parliamentary companion, 1901—*.
     1901—. Inaugurated in 1832, the latest volume (the 161st ed.) was pub-
     lished in 1974. Usually appears annually. Includes biographies of peers
     and members of the House of Commons, as well as names of public
     officials.

79   Ford, Percy and Grace. *A breviate of parliamentary papers, 1900—16*.
     Oxford, 1957. *1917—39*. Oxford, 1951. *1940—54*. Oxford, 1961.

80   —— and Diana Marshallsay. *Select list of parliamentary papers, 1955—1964*.
     Shannon, Ireland, 1970.

81   *Gazetteer of Great Britain: giving the position of all the names shown on the
     Ordnance Survey quarter-inch maps in terms of the national grid*.
     Chessington, 1953.

82   *General index to the bills, reports and papers printed by order of the House
     of Commons and to the reports and papers presented by command 1900
     to 1948—9*. H.M.S.O., 1960.

83   Golding, Louis. *Dictionary of local government in England and Wales*. 1962.

84   Grove, George. *Dictionary of music and musicians*, ed. Eric Blom. 5th ed.,
     1954, 9 vols. *Supplementary volume*, ed. Eric Blom. 1961.

85   *Guide to the contents of the Public Record Office*. 1963—8, 3 vols. Replaces
     M.S. Giuseppi, *A guide to the manuscripts preserved in the Public Record
     Office*. 1923—4, 2 vols.

86   *Guide to the historical publications of the societies of England and Wales*
     (*BIHR*, supplements I—XIII). 1929—46.

87   Hall, Hubert. *British archives and the sources for the history of the World
     War*. 1925.

88   Halsey, Albert H. (ed.). *Trends in British society since 1900*. 1972. Statisti-
     cal tables with detailed informed commentary.

89   Hazlehurst, Cameron and Christine Woodland. *A guide to the papers of
     British Cabinet ministers 1900—1951* (Royal Historical Society: Guides
     and Handbooks, Supplementary Series, no. 1). 1974. Locates and
     describes.

90   *Historical abstracts 1775—1945: bibliography of the world's periodical litera-
     ture*. Santa Barbara, Cal., 1955—. A quarterly assembled in annual vol-
     umes, providing a useful indexing service; author and subject indexes.

91   Historical Manuscripts Commission. *Record repositories in Great Britain*. 5th
     ed., 1973. Informs the researcher 'where the record material available . . .
     may be found, and what organisations will help him to approach and use
     it'.

92   Irwin, Raymond and Ronald Staveley (eds.). *The libraries of London*. 2nd
     ed., 1961. Outlines their resources.

93   *Jane's Fighting Ships, 1972—73*. 1973. The most recent volume in a long
     series; title and editorship vary. Indispensable for studying the British
     navy.
94   Kendall, M.G. (ed.). *The sources and nature of the statistics of the United
     Kingdom*. 1952—7, 2 vols. A reprint of articles in the *Journal of the Royal
     Statistical Society* beginning in 1949; constitutes a general guide for stat-
     istics on all aspects of British life.
95   Lloyd, John E. *et al.* (eds.). *The dictionary of Welsh biography down to 1940*.
     1959.
96   London and Cambridge Economic Service. *Key statistics of the British econ-
     omy 1900—1966*. N.d. Excellent for quick reference; somewhat limited.
97   *McCalmont's parliamentary poll book: British election results 1832—1918*,
     ed. John Vincent and Michael Stenton. 8th ed., Brighton, 1971. Includes
     by-elections 1910—18.
98   MacLeod, Roy M. *et al. The Corresponding Societies of the British Associ-
     ation for the Advancement of Science, 1883—1922*. 1974. Identifies and
     locates records.
99   Mitchell, Brian R. and Phyllis Deane. *Abstract of British historical statistics*.
     Cambridge, 1971. To 1938; supplemented by (100).
100 Mitchell, B.R. and H.G. Jones. *Second abstract of British historical statistics*.
     Cambridge, 1971. With (99) a standard reference.
101 Mitchell, Jean B. (ed.). *Great Britain: geographical essays*. Cambridge, 1962.
     Authoritative; fascinating for study of a particular region.
102 Morgan, Paul. *Oxford libraries outside the Bodleian: a guide*. Oxford, 1973.
103 Munby, Alan N.L. *Cambridge college libraries: aids for research students*. 2nd
     ed., Cambridge, 1962.
104 National Film Library. *Catalog*: I, *Silent News Films 1895—1933*. 2nd ed.,
     1965.
105 *The New York Times obituaries index, 1858—1968*. New York, 1970.
106 Ollard, Sidney L. *et al.* (eds.). *A dictionary of English church history*. 3rd ed.,
     1948.
107 Palmer, Samuel *et al.* (eds.). *Palmer's index to 'The Times' newspaper
     (London) 1790—1941*. Corsham, 1868—1943. Quarterly volumes. Kraus
     reprint, Vaduz, 1965—6, 82 vols.
108 PEP (Political and Economic Planning). This 'independent, non-party organis-
     ation', inaugurated in 1931, has published some 50 books and 500 broad-
     sheets. For a listing, see *Annual report 1969—1970*. N.d. 'A bridge be-
     tween research . . . and policy making'.
109 Pine, Leslie G. *The new extinct peerage, 1884—1971, containing extinct,
     abeyant, dormant and suspended peerages with genealogies and arms*.
     Baltimore, Md., 1973.
110 Powicke, F. Maurice and E.B. Fryde (eds.). *Handbook of British chronology*.
     2nd ed., 1961.
111 Public Record Office Handbooks. H.M.S.O. Include: No. 4, *List of Cabinet
     Papers, 1880—1914*. 1964. No. 6, *List of papers of the Committee of
     Imperial Defence, to 1914*. 1964. No. 9, *List of Cabinet Papers, 1915 and
     1916*. 1966. No. 10, *Classes of departmental papers for 1906—1939*.
     1966. No. 11, *The records of the Cabinet Office to 1922*. 1966. No. 13,
     The records of the Foreign Office 1782—1939*. 1969. No. 14, *Records of
     interest to social scientists 1919—1939, introduction*. 1971. No. 15, *The
     Second World War, a guide to documents in the Public Record Office*.
     1972.
112 Royal Society of London. *Biographical memoirs of the fellows of the Royal
     Society*. Vol. I—. 1955—. Latest vol. is XIX (1973). Continues *Obituary
     notices of fellows of the Royal Society*. 1932—54, 9 vols.
113 Scholes, Percy A. *The concise Oxford dictionary of music*, ed. John Owen
     Ward. 2nd ed., 1964. Condenses, with additional entries, Percy A. Scholes.
     Oxford companion to music. 1938.
114 Stamp, L. Dudley and Stanley H. Beaver. *The British Isles: a geographic and
     economic survey*. 5th ed., 1963.
115 *The statesman's year book: statistical and historical annual of the states of*

the world. 1864—. 109th ed. was published in 1972. Invaluable for quick reference.

116   *Statistical abstract of the United Kingdom.* 1856—. Succeeded by *Annual abstract of statistics.* 1948—. Issued by Central Statistical Office.

117   Steinberg, Sigfrid H. and I.H. Evans (eds.). *Steinberg's dictionary of British history.* 2nd ed., 1971.

118   Stewart, James D. *et al.* (eds.). *British union catalogue of periodicals: a record of the periodicals of the world from the seventeenth century to the present day in British libraries.* 1955—8, 4 vols. Supplementary volumes (title slightly changed) with titles of new periodicals. 1962—.

119   *The subject index to periodicals.* 1915—61. Quarterly since 1954. From 1962 known as *British humanities index.* 1962—. The best guide to articles on British history.

120   *The Times,* London. *Annual index to The Times 1906—.* 1907—. Place of publication varies. In 1914 the title changes to *The official index.* More complete than (107); available on film.

121   *The Times guide to the House of Commons 1970.* 1970. The latest volume in a series which has appeared after each General Election since 1900. Title varies slightly; includes biographies of M.P.'s as well as results of the polls.

122   *Urban history yearbook 1974,* ed. H.J. Dyos. Leicester, 1974. The first volume in a venture 'planned to advance the further development of urban history'. Includes reports on conferences, reviews, bibliographies, register of research in progress.

123   Vogel, Robert. *A breviate of British diplomatic blue books 1919—1939.* 1963. Continues Temperley, Harold W.V. and Lillian M. Penson. *A century of diplomatic blue books, 1814—1914.* Cambridge, 1938.

124   Whitaker, Joseph. *An almanack for the year of our Lord . . . 1901—.* 1901—. Annual; known generally as *Whitaker's almanac*; the 106th ed. appeared in 1974; the most useful book of reference for Britain and the Commonwealth.

125   Whitmore, John B. *A genealogical guide: an index to British pedigrees in continuation of Marshall's Genealogist's Guide (1903).* 1947—53, 4 parts.

126   *Who's who 1973—1974: an annual biographical dictionary.* Indispensable for contemporary biography. See also *Who was who.* 1919—72, 6 vols. Embraces 1897—1970.

127   Williams, Trevor I. (ed.). *A biographical dictionary of scientists.* 1969.

128   *Willing's press guide 1973.* 1973. Annual since 1899.

III. GENERAL SURVEYS

129   Furth, Charles. *Life since 1900.* 3rd ed., 1966. Popular essay.

130   Gilbert, Bentley B. *Britain since 1918.* 1967. Especially good on social welfare.

131   Havighurst, Alfred F. *Twentieth-century Britain.* 2nd ed., New York, 1966. A third edition is in progress.

132   Lloyd, Trevor O. *Empire to welfare state: English history 1906—1967.* Oxford, 1970.

133   Lyons, Francis S.L. *Ireland since the famine.* New York, 1971.

134   Marriott, John A.R. *Modern England, 1885—1945: a history of my own times.* 4th ed., 1960.

135   Medlicott, William N. *Contemporary England 1914—1964.* 1967.

136   Meech, Thomas Cox. *This generation: a history of Great Britain and Ireland from 1900 to 1926.* 1927—8, 2 vols.

137   Mowat, Charles Loch. *Britain between the wars 1918—1940.* 1955.

138   Pelling, Henry. *Modern Britain, 1885—1955.* 1960.

139   Pryde, George S. *Scotland from 1603 to the present day,* II. 1962.

140   Reynolds, Ernest E. and Norman H. Brasher. *Britain in the twentieth century 1900—1964.* Cambridge, 1966.

141   Seaman, Lewis C.B. *Post-Victorian Britain 1902—1951.* 1966.

142 Somervell, David C. *Modern Britain 1870–1950*. 9th ed., 1960.
143 Spender, John A. *Great Britain: empire and commonwealth, 1886–1935*. 1936. In its day one of the best treatments; liberal perspective.
144 Taylor, Alan J.P. *English History 1914–1945* (Oxford History of England, XV). Oxford, 1965. Its brilliance more than compensates for an occasional error. For a general survey of 1901–1914, see the previous volume in the Oxford History, Ensor, R.C.K. *England 1870–1914*. Oxford, 1936;
145 Thomson, David. *England in the twentieth century* (Pelican History of England, IX). 1965.

IV. CONSTITUTIONAL AND ADMINISTRATIVE HISTORY

1 Printed sources

146 Amery, Leopold S. *Thoughts on the constitution*. 2nd ed., 1953. Based on Amery's Chichele Lectures, 1946; by an articulate and independent Conservative.
147 Beaverbrook, William Maxwell Aitken, 1st Baron. *Abdication of King Edward VIII*, ed. Alan J.P. Taylor. 1966.
148 Cumpston, Ina M. (ed.). *The growth of the British Commonwealth 1880– 1932*. 1973. Documents with commentary.
149 Dawson, Robert MacGregor (ed.). *The development of Dominion status 1900–1936*. 1937. Documents with commentary.
150 Garbett, Cyril F. *Church and state in England*. 1950. The Archbishop of York argues for readjustment; much reference to twentieth-century development.
151 Grover, B.L. *A documentary study of British policy toward Indian nationalism, 1885–1909*. Delhi, 1967.
152 Halsbury, Hardinge Stanley Giffard, 1st Earl of. *Halsbury's laws of England*. Various editions from 1900 to the present. Often known as 'Halsbury's statutes of England'.
153 Hanson, Albert H. and Herbert Victor Wiseman. *Parliament at work: a casebook of parliamentary procedure*. 1962. In the main, on period after 1945.
154 Hardinge, Helen Mary. *Loyal to three kings*. 1967. A memoir of Alec Hardinge, principal private secretary to Edward VIII; usefor for abdication crisis.
155 Keir, David Lindsay and F.H. Lawson (eds.). *Cases in constitutional law*, 5th ed., 1967. A standard collection.
156 Laski, Harold. *Reflections on the constitution: the House of Commons, the Cabinet, the Civil Service*. New York, 1951.
157 *The law reports . . . ; ten years digest 1901 to 1910; all the cases reported in the Law Reports and in the Weekly Notes*. 1911. Continues for ten and twenty year periods.
158 Le May, Godfrey H.L. *British government, 1914–1953: select documents*. 1955. A very useful collection; no commentary.
159 Lowther, James William, 1st Viscount Ullswater. *A Speaker's commentaries*. 1925, 2 vols.
160 Mansergh, Nicholas (ed.). *Documents and speeches on Commonwealth affairs 1931–1952*. 1953, 2 vols. *1952–1962*. 1963.
161 Morrison, Herbert, Baron Morrison of Lambeth. *Government and parliament: a survey from the inside*. 2nd ed., 1959. By a prominent Labour leader.
162 *The parliamentary debates, 1900–1908*. 1900–8. Lords and Commons are together.
163 *The parliamentary debates: House of Lords*. 1909–.
164 *The parliamentary debates: House of Commons*. 1909–;
165 Perham, Margery F. *Colonial sequence, 1930–1949: a chronological com-*

mentary upon British colonial policy especially in Africa. 1967. 'Occasional writings' from various sources. Continued by *Colonial sequence, 1949–1969*. 1970.

166   Ponsonby, Frederick, 1st Lord Syonsby, *Recollections of three reigns*, ed. Colin Welch. 1952. Court life under Victoria, Edward VII and George V.

167   *The public general statutes of the United Kingdom of Great Britain and Ireland. 1866–1947*. Public acts of each parliamentary session.

168   Stephenson, Carl and Frederick George Marcham (eds.). *Sources of English constitutional history*. Rev. ed., 1972, 2 vols. Vol II: *A selection of documents from the Interregnum to the present*. Fundamental documents.

169   Windsor, Duke of. *A king's story: memoirs of the Duke of Windsor*. New York, 1957. Concerning his abdication.

170   Wiseman, Herbert Victor. *Parliament and the executive: an analysis with readings*. 1966.

2 Surveys

171   Bradley, Kenneth B. *The living Commonwealth*. 1961. Popular survey, worth reading.

172   Campion, Gilbert F.M. *et al. British government since 1918*. 1950.

173   Chester, Daniel N. (ed.). *The organisation of British central government 1914–1956*. 1957. A survey by a study group at the Royal Institute of Public Administration.

174   Gordon, Donald C. *The moment of power: Britain's imperial epoch*. Englewood Cliffs, N.J., 1970. A survey, well informed, interpretative; emphasis on India. Cf. Cross, Colin. *The fall of the British Empire, 1918–1968*. 1968.

175   Keir, David Lindsay. *The constitutional history of modern Britain since 1485*. 6th ed., 1960.

176   Keith, Arthur Berriedale. *The constitution of England from Victoria to George VI*. 1940, 2 vols.

177   Knaplund, Paul. *Commonwealth and empire 1901–1955*. 1956.

178   Plucknett, Theodore F.T. *A concise history of the common law*. 5th ed., 1956. The best brief history.

179   Redlich, Josef and Francis W. Hirst. *The history of local government in England*, ed. Bryan Keith-Lucas. 2nd ed., 1970. Brief summary on twentieth century.

180   Robson, William A. *The development of local government*. 3rd ed., 1954.

181   Rose, J. Holland *et al.* (eds.). *Cambridge History of the British Empire*, VI, *Canada and Newfoundland*, VII, *Australia, New Zealand*. Cambridge, 1930, 1933.

182   Smellie, Kingsley B. *A history of local government*. 4th ed., 1968. Largely on twentieth century; takes the story to 1965.

183   ——— *A hundred years of English government*. 2nd ed., 1950. Takes the story to 1949.

184   Taswell-Langmead, Thomas Pitt. *English constitutional history from the teutonic conquest to the present time*, ed. Theodore F.T. Plucknett. 10th ed., 1946.

185   Walker, Eric A. (ed.). *The Cambridge history of the British Empire*, VIII, *South Africa, Rhodesia and the High Commission territories*. 2nd ed., Cambridge, 1963. Chapters by various authors.

3 Monographs
(See also sec. V, pt. 3, below.)

186   Abel-Smith, Brian and Robert Stevens. *Lawyers and the courts: a sociological study of the English legal system, 1750–1965*. 1967.

187   Abramovitz, Moses and Vera F. Eliasberg. *The growth of public employment in Great Britain*. Princeton, N.J., 1957.

188   Allyn, Emily. *Lords versus Commons: a century of conflict and compromise, 1830–1930*. New York, 1931.

189   Bell, Philip M.H. *Disestablishment in Ireland and Wales*. 1969.

190   Beloff, Max. *Imperial sunset*, I, *Britain's liberal empire 1897—1921*. 1969.

191   Benewick, Robert. *The Fascist movement in Britain*. Rev. ed., 1972. First published in 1969 as *Political violence and public disorder*.

192   Berkeley, Humphry. *The power of the prime minister*. 1968. Develops the thesis that 'prime ministerial government' replaced cabinet government under Lloyd George. See also (305).

193   Bishop, Donald G. *The administration of British foreign relations*. Syracuse, N.Y., 1961.

194   Blom-Cooper, Louis J. and Gavin Drewry. *Final appeal: a study of the House of Lords in its judicial capacity*. 1972.

195   Brittan, Samuel. *The Treasury under the Tories 1951—1964*. 1964.

196   Broad, C. Lewis. *The abdication: twenty five years after: a reappraisal*. 1961.

197   Bromhead, Peter A. *The House of Lords and contemporary politics 1911—1957*. 1958.

198   —— *Private members' bills in the British parliament*. 1956.

199   Browne, Douglas G. *The rise of Scotland Yard: a history of the Metropolitan Police*. 1956.

200   Buck, Philip W. *Amateurs and professionals in British politics, 1918—1959*. Chicago, Ill., 1963. Based on interviews and statistics.

201   Buckland, Patrick. *Irish unionism*, I, *The Anglo-Irish and the new Ireland, 1885—1922*; II, *Ulster Unionism and the origins of Northern Ireland 1886—1922*. Dublin, 1972—3.

202   Bulmer-Thomas, Ivor. *The growth of the British party system*. 2nd ed., New York, 1967, 2 vols.

203   Chester, Daniel N. and Nona Bowring. *Questions in parliament*. Oxford, 1962. A historical treatment.

204   Christoph, James B. *Capital punishment and British politics: the British movement to abolish the death penalty 1945—57*. 1962.

205   Coombes, David L. *The member of parliament and the administration: the case of the Select Committee on Nationalized Industries*. 1966. On developments since 1956.

206   Daalder, Hans. *Cabinet reform in Britain, 1914—1963*. Stanford, Cal., 1963.

207   Davies, Joseph. *The prime minister's secretariat, 1916—1920*. Newport, Monmouthshire, 1951. The author was a member of the secretariat.

208   Dicey, Albert V. *Introduction to the study of the law of the constitution*. 10th ed., with an introduction by E.C.S. Wade, 1959. A classic; the new introduction is relevant to the twentieth century.

209   Eaves, John. *Emergency powers and the parliamentary watchdog: parliament and the executive in Great Britain, 1939—1951*. 1957.

210   Edwards, Owen Dudley *et al. Celtic nationalism*. 1968.

211   Ehrman, John. *Cabinet government and war, 1890—1940*. Cambridge, 1958. See also (297).

212   Emden, Cecil S. *The people and the constitution: being a history of the development of the people's influence in British government*. 2nd ed., Oxford, 1956.

213   Fawcett, James E.S. *The British Commonwealth in international affairs*. 1963.

214   Fox, Lionel W. *The English prisons and Borstal systems*. 1952. Since the Criminal Justice Act (1948), with historical introduction.

215   Fraser, Robert (ed.). *The new Whitehall series*. 1955—70, 14 vols. 'To provide authoritative descriptions of the present work of the major departments of the Central Government.' The volumes include: Newsam, Frank, *The Home Office*. 1954. Strang, William, 1st Baron, *The Foreign Office*. 1955. King, Geoffrey, *The Ministry of Pensions and National Insurance*. 1958. Ince, Godfrey, *The Ministry of Labour and National Service*. 1960. Bridges, Edward E., Baron, *The Treasury*. 2nd ed., 1966. Clark, Fife, *The Central Office of Information*. 1970.

216   Fry, Geoffrey Kingdon. *Statesmen in disguise: the changing role of the administrative class of the British home civil service 1853—1966*. 1969.

217   Gallagher, Frank. *The indivisible island: the history of the partition of Ireland*. 1957. Readable; well-documented.

218   Gann, Lewis H. and Peter Duignan *et al.* (eds.). *Colonialism in Africa, 1870–1960*. 1969–73. 5 vols. Excellent chapters on Britain's role.

219   Gilmour, Ian. *The body politic*. 1969. History used to bolster ideas about the English constitution.

220   Ginsberg, Morris (ed.). *Law and opinion in England in the 20th century*. 1959.

221   Gordon, Donald C. *The Dominion partnership in imperial defense 1870–1914*. Baltimore, Md., 1965.

222   Gordon, Lincoln. *The public corporation in Great Britain*. 1938. In historical context.

223   Gordon-Walker, Patrick. *The Commonwealth*. 1962. Perceptive treatment of historical development.

224   Hamilton, William B. *et al.* (eds.). *A decade of the Commonwealth 1955–1964*. 1966. By various authors.

225   Hancock, William Keith. *Survey of Commonwealth affairs*; I, *Problems of nationality, 1918–1936*; II, *Problems of economic policy, 1918–1939*. 1937–42.

226   Hanham, Harold J. *Scottish nationalism*. 1969. Detailed historical context.

227   Hansard Society. *Parliamentary reform, 1933–60: a survey of suggested reforms*. 1961.

228   Hardie, Frank M. *The political influence of the British monarchy 1868–1952*. New York, 1970. Extension of *The political influence of Queen Victoria, 1861–1901*. 1935. Eminently readable.

229   Hart, Jenifer M. *The British police*. 1951. Informative.

230   Heussler, Robert. *Yesterday's rulers: the making of the British colonial service*. Syracuse, N.Y., 1963. 'A study of the methods of recruitment and training of colonial administrators', 1920–45.

231   Hicks, Ursula K. *British public finances: their structure and development, 1880–1952*. 1954. See also (559).

232   Hodson, Henry V. *The great divide: Britain, India, Pakistan*. 1970. Informed, well written, popular.

233   Howe, Roland. *The story of Scotland Yard: a history of the C.I.D. from the earliest times to the present day*. 1965. Popular account.

234   Inglis, Brian. *Abdication*. New York, 1966. Concerning Edward VIII. See also (147, 262).

235   Jackson, Richard Meredith. *The machinery of justice in England*. 2nd ed., Cambridge, 1953. With considerable historical reference.

236   Jenkins, Roy H. *Mr Balfour's poodle: an account of the struggle between the House of Lords and the government of Mr Asquith*. 1954.

237   Jennings, W. Ivor. *Cabinet government*. 3rd ed., Cambridge, 1959. A thorough study in a historical context.

238   —— *Party politics*, I, *Appeal to the people*; II, *The growth of parties*; III, *The stuff of parties*. Cambridge, 1960–2.

239   —— *Parliament*. 2nd ed., Cambridge, 1957.

240   Johnson, Franklyn Arthur. *Defence by committee: the British Committee of Imperial Defence, 1885–1959*. 1960.

241   Johnson, Nevil. *Parliament and administration: the estimates committee 1945–65*. 1966.

242   Keith, A. Berriedale. *The king and the imperial crown: the powers and duties of His Majesty*. 1936.

243   —— *The king, the constitution, the Empire and foreign affairs: letters and essays, 1936–7*. 1938.

244   Kendle, John Edward. *The colonial and imperial conferences, 1887–1911: a study in imperial organization*. 1967.

245   Mansergh, Nicholas. *The Commonwealth experience*. New York, 1969. General treatment.

246   Mansergh, Nicholas and E.W.R. Lumby (eds.). *Constitutional relations between Britain and India: the transfer of power 1942–7*. 1970–3, 4 vols.

247   Mansergh, Nicholas. *Survey of British Commonwealth affairs: problems of external policy 1931–1939*. 1952.

248   —— *Survey of British Commonwealth affairs: problems of wartime co-operation and post-war change 1939–1952*. 1958.

249   Martin, John P. and Gail Wilson. *The police: a study in manpower: the evolution of the service in England and Wales, 1829–1965.* 1969. Reliable.

250   Martin, Kingsley. *The crown and the establishment.* 1962. Essays analysing the monarchy in the twentieth century. See also his earlier work, *The magic of monarchy.* 1936.

251   Martindale, Hilda. *Women servants of the state 1870–1938.* 1938. On women in civil service.

252   Morris, Homer Lawrence. *Parliamentary franchise reform in England from 1885 to 1918* (Studies in History, Economics and Public Law, Columbia University, XCVI, no. 2). New York, 1921.

253   Pandey, Bishwa N. *The break-up of British India.* 1969. General study, 1900–1947.

254   Paton, Herbert J. *The claim of Scotland.* 1968. 'The claim of Scotland to govern herself' is treated in the context of recent history.

255   Peacock, Alan T. and Jack Wiseman. *The growth of public expenditure in the United Kingdom.* Princeton, N.J., 1961. Considers developments since 1890.

256   Pyrah, Geoffrey B. *Imperial policy and South Africa 1902–1910.* Oxford, 1955.

257   Reese, Trevor R. *The history of the Royal Commonwealth Society, 1868–1968.* Oxford, 1968.

258   Reynolds, Gerald W. and Anthony Judge. *The night the police went on strike.* 1968. Events of 1918–19.

259   Robson, William A. (ed.). *The civil service in Britain and France.* 1956. By various writers; more British than French.

260   Rose, Gordon. *The struggle for penal reform.* 1961.

261   Ross, James Frederick Stanley. *Elections and electors.* 1955. Critical study of parliamentary representation 1918–35 with proposals for reform.

262   Sencourt, Robert. *The reign of Edward VIII.* 1962. See also (234) and Donaldson, Frances, *Edward VIII.* 1974.

263   Sparks, Richard F. *Local prisons: the crisis in the English penal system.* 1971. Based on studies in 1960s.

264   Thomas, John Alun. *The House of Commons, 1906–1911: an analysis of its economic and social character.* Cardiff, 1958.

265   Thompson, L.M. *The unification of South Africa, 1902–1910.* Oxford, 1960.

266   Vernon, Roland V. and Nicholas Mansergh. *Advisory bodies: a study of their uses in relation to central government, 1919–1939.* 1940.

267   Walker-Smith, Derek. *Lord Reading and his cases.* New York, 1934. Lord Reading was lord chief justice 1913–21.

268   Wang, Chi Kao. *Dissolution of the British parliament 1832–1931.* New York, 1934.

269   Wheare, Kenneth C. *The constitutional structure of the Commonwealth.* Oxford, 1960.

270   —— *The statute of Westminster and Dominion status.* 5th ed., 1953. Concerns the statute of 1931.

271   Wickwar, W. Hardy. *The public services: a historical survey.* 1938.

272   Williams, David. *Keeping the peace: the police and public order.* 1967. Excellent general treatment.

273   Williamson, James A. *A notebook of Commonwealth history.* 3rd ed., 1967. Excellent for reference.

274   Wilson, Monica and Leonard Thompson (eds.). *The Oxford history of South Africa,* II, *South Africa 1870–1966.* 1971.

4 Biographies

275   Battiscombe, Georgina. *Queen Alexandra.* 1969.

276   Birkenhead, Frederick W.F. Smith, 2nd Earl of. *Walter Monckton: the life of Viscount Monckton of Brenchley.* 1969. Excellent on Edward VIII.

277   Duff, David. *Elizabeth of Glamis.* 1973. Biography of the present queen mother.

278 Fox, A. Wilson. *The Earl of Halsbury, lord high chancellor (1823–1921)*. 1929.
279 Gore, John. *King George V, a personal memoir*. 1941.
280 Heuston, Robert F.V. *Lives of the lord chancellors, 1885–1940*. Oxford, 1964.
281 Hyde, H. Montgomery. *Norman Birkett: the life of Lord Birkett of Ulverston*. 1964.
282 Jackson, Robert. *The chief: the biography of Gordon Hewart, lord chief justice of England, 1922–40*. 1959.
283 Lee, Sidney. *King Edward VII*, II, *The reign*. New York, 1927.
284 Magnus, Philip. *King Edward the seventh*. 1964. The best biography.
285 Nicolson, Harold. *King George the fifth: his life and reign*. 1952. One of the best royal biographies.
286 Pope-Hennessy, James. *Queen Mary 1867–1953*. 1959.
287 Wheeler-Bennett, John W. *King George VI: his life and reign*. 1958.

5 Articles
(See also sec. V, pt. 5, below.)

288 Beaglehole, John C. 'The British Commonwealth of nations', *NCMH*, 373–402. A general essay.
289 Berry, C.L. 'The coronation oath and the Church of England', *Journal of Ecclesiastical History*, XI (April 1960), 98–105.
290 Bromhead, Peter A. 'Mr Wedgwood Benn, the peerage and the constitution', *Parliamentary Affairs*, XIV (Autumn 1961), 493–506. A constitutional problem ending with the Peerage Act of 1963.
291 Browett, Leonard. 'Road administration', *PA*, XVII (Jan. 1939), 32–46.
292 Butler, David. 'The redistribution of seats', *PA* XXXIII (summer 1955), 125–47. A consideration of the background of the redistribution in 1955.
293 Caldwell, J.A.M. 'The genesis of the Ministry of Labour', *PA*, XXXVII (winter 1959), 367–91.
294 Chester, Daniel N. 'Management and accountability in the nationalised industries', *PA*, XXX (spring 1952), 27–47.
295 Dodd, C.H. 'Recruitment to the administrative class 1960–1964', *PA*, XLV (Spring 1967), 55–80.
296 Ehrman, John. 'Lloyd George and Churchill as war ministers', *TRHS*, 5th ser., XI (1961), 101–15. A valuable comparative treatment.
297 Finer, Herman. 'The British Cabinet, the House of Commons and the war', *Political Science Quarterly*, LVI (Sept. 1941), 321–60.
298 Hardie, Frank. 'The king and the constitutional crisis', *History Today*, XX (May 1970), 338–47.
299 Hyam, Ronald R. 'Smuts and the decision of the Liberal Government to grant responsible government to the Transvaal, January and February 1906', *Hist. J.*, VIII (no. 3, 1965), 380–98. See also Gilbert, B.B. 'The grant of responsible government to the Transvaal: more notes on a myth', *Hist. J.*, X (no. 4, 1967), 457–9.
300 Kellas, James G. 'The Liberal Party and the Scottish Church disestablishment crisis', *EHR*, LXXIX (Jan. 1964), 31–46.
301 Kermode, D.G. 'Legislative–executive relationship in the Isle of Man', *PS*, XVI (1968), 18–42. Developments since 1957.
302 MacGregor, J.J. 'Recent land-tenure changes in mid-Devon', *Economica*, new ser., I (no. 4, 1934), 459–72.
303 Mackintosh, John P. 'The role of the Committee of Imperial Defence before 1914', *EHR*, LXXVII (July 1962), 490–503.
304 Moodie, Graeme C. 'The monarch and the selection of a prime minister: a re-examination of the crisis of 1931', *PS*, V (1957), 1–20. See (470).
305 Morgan, Kenneth O. 'Lloyd George's premiership: a study in prime ministerial government', *Hist. J.*, XIII (no. 1, 1970), 130–57.
306 —— 'Welsh nationalism: the historical background', *JCH*, VI (no. 1, 1971), 153–72.

307 Naylor, John F. 'The establishment of the Cabinet secretarist', *Hist. J.*, XIV (no. 4, 1971), 783–803.
308 Nottage, Raymond and Freida Stack. 'The Royal Institute of Public Administration 1922–1939', *PA*, L (Autumn 1971), 281–302. Continued by Nottage, Raymond. 'The Royal Institute of Public Administration 1939–1972', *PA*, L (Winter 1971), 419–46.
309 Rose, Gordon. 'Trends in the development of criminology in Britain', *BJS*, IX (March 1958), 53–65.
310 Ross, James Frederick Stanley. 'Women and parliamentary elections', *BJS*, IV (1953), 14–24.
311 Weston, Corinne Comstock. 'The Liberal leadership and the Lords' veto, 1907–1910', *Hist. J.*, XI (no. 3, 1968), 508–37.
312 Wilding, Paul. 'The administrative aspects of the 1918 housing scheme', *PA*, LI (Autumn 1973), 307–23.
313 Willson, F.M.G. 'The routes of entry of new members of the British Cabinet 1868–1958', *PS*, VII (no. 3, 1959), 222–32.
314 Willson, F.M.G. 'The organisation of British central government 1955–1961', *PA*, XL (Summer 1962), 159–206.
315 Wiseman, Herbert Victor. 'Regional government in the United Kingdom', *Parliamentary Affairs*, XIX (winter 1965–6), 56–82. A historical treatment, largely after 1940.
316 Wolf-Phillips, Leslie, 'Post-independence constitutional change in the Commonwealth', *PS*, XVIII (1970), 18–42.

V. POLITICAL HISTORY

1 Printed sources
(See also sec. IV, pt. 1, above.)

317 Addison, Christopher. *Four and a half years: a personal diary from Jume 1914 to January 1919*. 1934, 2 vols. By a prominent officer of state.
318 —— *Politics from within, 1911–1918*. 1924, 2 vols.
319 Amery, Leopold. *My political life*. 1953–5, 3 vols. By a statesman prominent in the twenties.
320 Askwith, George Ranken, 1st Baron. *Industrial problems and disputes*. 1920. By a noted industrial conciliator, 1911–19.
321 Asquith, Herbert Henry, 1st Earl of Oxford and Asquith. *Fifty years of parliament*. 1926, 2 vols. A personal history.
322 —— *Letters of the Earl of Oxford and Asquith to a friend* [ed. Desmond MacCarthy]. 1933–4, 2 vols.
323 —— *Memories and reflections, 1852–1927*. Boston, 1928, 2 vols.
324 Asquith, Margot. *An autobiography*. New York, 1920, 2 vols. Fascinating if not always reliable. Continued by *More memories*. 1933.
325 Attlee, Clement, Earl Attlee. *As it happened*. 1954. A disappointing autobiography, especially on domestic affairs. Attlee is more perceptive in his *The Labour Party in perspective*. 1937.
326 Barker, Bernard (ed.). *Ramsay MacDonald's political writings*. 1972. MacDonald's views on British socialism.
327 Barnes, George N. *From workshop to War Cabinet*. 1924. By a labour leader, prominent 1906–22.
328 Bealey, Frank. 'Negotiations between the Liberal Party and the Labour Representation Committee before the General Election of 1906', *BIHR*, XXIX (1956), 261–74. Documents.
329 Bealey, Frank (ed.). *The social and political thought of the British Labour Party*. 1970. Extracts from one hundred speeches and writings, 1900–67.
330 Beattie, Alan (ed.). *English party politics*, II, *The twentieth century*. 1970. Documents with commentary.
331 [Begbie, Harold]. *The mirrors of Downing Street: some political reflections*

By a Gentleman with a Duster. 1920. A contemporary comment on thirteen leaders.

332 Bevan, Aneurin. *In place of fear*. New ed., 1961. First published in 1952; a statement of Bevan's political and social philosophy.

333 Birrell, Augustine. *Things past redress*. 1937. Autobiography.

334 Blatchford, Robert. *My eighty years*. 1931. By a talented journalist and ardent Socialist.

335 Block, Geoffrey D.M. *A source book of Conservatism*. 1964. Interesting essays on out of the way subjects; good bibliography.

336 Blunt, Wilfrid Scawen. *My diaries, being a personal narrative of events 1884—1914*. New York, 1921. By a brilliant conversationalist and man of letters.

337 Boothby, Robert J.G., Baron Boothby. *I fight to live*. 1947. Autobiographical from 1919 to 1941. By a Conservative supporter of Churchill in the 1930s. See also his *My yesterday, your tomorrow* (1962) for essays based on his lectures, speeches and articles.

338 Braddock, Jack and Bessie. *The Braddocks*. 1963. Reminiscences of socialist, communist and labour associations.

339 Briggs, Asa (ed.). *They saw it happen*, IV, *an anthology of eye-witnesses' accounts of events in British history, 1897—1940*. Oxford, 1960.

340 Brockway, A. Fenner. *Inside the left: thirty years of platform, press, prison and parliament*. 1942. Autobiography of an Independent Labour Party leader; goes to 1939. For its sequel see *Outside the right*. 1963.

341 Brown, George, Baron George-Brown. *In my way*. 1970. Political memoirs of a Labour leader in the sixties.

342 Buchan, John, Baron Tweedsmuir. *Pilgrim's way*. Cambridge, Mass., 1940. Published in England as *Memory hold-the-door*. 1940. Autobiography of a noted author and governor-general of Canada. See also (765).

343 Bunbury, Henry N. (ed.). *Lloyd George's ambulance wagon; being the memoirs of William J. Braithwaite, 1911—1912*. 1957. 'The inside story of the preparation and passage through Parliament of the National Insurance Act of 1911' by a civil servant in the Inland Revenue Department.

344 Butler, Richard Austen, Baron. *The art of the possible: the memoirs of Lord Butler, K.G., C.H*. 1971. A fascinating and significant autobiography.

345 Cecil, Robert, 1st Viscount Cecil of Chelwood. *A great experiment: an autobiography*. New York, 1941. Significant in studying Britain and the League of Nations.

346 Chamberlain, Austen. *Down the years*. 1934. 'Random recollections' of men and events. See also his *Politics from the inside: an epistolary chronicle 1906—1914*. 1936.

347 Channon, Henry. *'Chips', the diaries of Sir Henry Channon*, ed. Robert Rhodes James. 1967. Selections from fascinating diaries of a leading social figure and an M.P., 1935—58.

348 Chirol, Valentine. *Fifty years in a changing world*. 1927. Autobiography.

349 Churchill, Randolph S. and Martin Gilbert. *Winston S. Churchill, companion volumes*, I—III. Boston, Mass., 1967—73. These volumes of documents, 1874—1916, accompany (685) in progress.

350 Churchill, Winston Spencer. *His complete speeches 1897—1963*, ed. Robert Rhodes James. New York, 1974, 8 vols. The definitive collection. But for some speeches outside parliament only extracts are given; consult (351, 353).

351 —— *Liberalism and the social problem*. 1909. Collected speeches, 1906—9.

352 —— *Secret session speeches*, compiled by Charles Eade. 1946. Five speeches during World WAR II not recorded at the time.

353 —— *The war speeches of the Rt. Hon. Winston S. Churchill*, ed. Charles Eade. 1951—2, 3 vols.

354 —— *The world crisis, 1914—1918*. New York, 1923—7, 4 vols. Copious documents.

355 —— *The aftermath (the world crisis 1918—1928)*. New York, 1929. Includes documents.

356 Clynes, John R. *Memoirs*. 1937, 2 vols. Unexciting but useful account of a respected Labour leader.
357 Cockburn, Claud. *In time of trouble: an autobiography*. 1956. Continued in his *Crossing the line*. 1958. Interesting presentation of Communist attitudes.
358 Cole, Margaret. *Growing up into revolution*. 1949. Rambling reminiscences of the Labour movement and Fabianism.
359 *Constitutional year book*. See (423).
360 Cooper, Duff, 1st Viscount Norwich. *Old men forget*. 1953.
361 Craig, Frederick W.S. (ed.). *British General Election manifestos 1918–1966*. Chichester, 1970.
362 Crozier, William P. *Off the record: political interviews 1933–1943*, ed. Alan J.P. Taylor. 1973. The editor of the *Manchester Guardian* interviews leading political figures.
363 Cummings, [Michael]. *These uproarious years: a pictorial post-war history, with an introduction by Hugh Massingham*. 1954. Cartoons from the *Daily Express*.
364 Dalton, Hugh. *Call back yesterday: memoirs, 1887–1931*. 1953. *The fateful years: memoirs, 1931–45*. 1957. *High tide and after: memoirs, 1945–1960*. 1962. Based on diaries; outstanding in significance.
365 Eccles, David McAdam, 1st Baron. *Life and politics: a moral diagnosis*. 1967.
366 Eden, Anthony. *The memoirs of Anthony Eden: full circle*. 1960. *Facing the dictators*. 1962. *The reckoning*. 1965. *Full circle* is essential for the Suez crisis, 1956.
367 Esher, Reginald Brett, 1st Viscount. *Journals and letters of Reginald Viscount Esher*, ed. Maurice V. Brett and Oliver Sylvain Baliol Brett, 3rd Viscount Esher. 1934–8, 4 vols. The last three volumes embrace 1903–30. See also (704).
368 Fawcett, Millicent Garrett. *The women's victory — and after: personal reminiscences, 1911–1918*. 1920. By a leader of the women's suffrage movement.
369 Fitzroy, Almeric. *Memoirs*. 6th ed. [1925], 2 vols. Spans 1898–1923.
370 Gallacher, William. *Revolt on the Clyde: an autobiography*. 1936. One of the best accounts of Communist politics. See also *The last memoirs of Willie Gallacher*. 1966.
371 Gilbert, Martin. *Plough my own furrow: the story of Lord Allen of Hurtwood as told through his writings and correspondence*. 1965.
372 —— (ed.). *Lloyd George*. Englewood Cliffs, N.J., 1968. Documents by and about Lloyd George.
373 Gooch, George P. *Under six reigns*. 1958. Reminiscence.
374 Graham, John W. *Conscription and conscience*, with a preface by Clifford Allen. 1971. Originally published in 1922; a reconstruction of the experiences of conscientious objectors.
375 Grigg, Percy J. *Prejudice and judgment*. 1948. By a civil servant (from 1913) and cabinet member.
376 Haldane, Richard Burdon, Viscount Haldane. *An autobiography*. New York, 1929.
377 —— *Before the war*. 1920. Haldane was war secretary 1905–12.
378 Halifax, Edward Frederick Lindley Wood, 1st Earl of. *Fulness of days*. 1957. Weak.
379 Hamilton, Mary Agnes. *Remembering my good friends*. 1944.
380 Hancock, William Keith and Jean Van der Poel (eds.). *Selections from the Smuts Papers*. Cambridge 1966–73, 7 vols. Incomplete. See (712).
381 Hewins, William A.S. *The apologia of an imperialist: forty years of empire policy*. 1929, 2 vols. By a political economist, historian and politician.
382 Hill, Charles, Baron. *Both sides of the hill*. 1964. 'Personal recollections.'
383 Hobson, Samuel G. *Pilgrim to the left: memoirs of a modern revolutionist*. 1938. By a Fabian and guild socialist.
384 James, Robert Rhodes (ed.). *Memoirs of a Conservative: J.C.C. Davidson's memoirs and papers, 1910–1937*. 1969. Especially useful for studying Baldwin.

385 Johnston, Thomas. *Memories*. 1951. Excellent on Labour and Scotland.
386 Jones, Thomas. *Whitehall Diary*, ed. Keith Middlemas. 1969—71, 3 vols. Embraces 1916—30.
387 —— *A diary with letters, 1931—1950*. 1954. One of the best political sources, especially useful on Cliveden set.
388 Kilmuir, D.P. Maxwell Fyfe, Earl of. *Political adventure: the memoirs of the Earl of Kilmuir*. 1964. By a Conservative politician and law officer of the crown.
389 [King, Cecil]. *The Cecil King Diary 1965—1970*. 1972. By a prominent newspaper proprietor.
390 Kirkwood, David. *My life of revolt*. 1935. Clydeside life and politics.
391 Labour Party. *Report of the . . . annual conference*. 1901—. Title varies slightly.
392 Labour Party. *The war aims of the British people*. [1918]. Adopted by the Joint Conference of the Labour Party and the Parliamentary Committee of the Trades Union Congress, 28 Dec. 1917.
393 *Labour [party] year book*. See (423).
394 Labour Representation Committee. *Conference on labour representation held . . . on Tuesday, the 27th February, 1900 . . .* [London, 1900].
395 Lansbury, George. *My life*. 1928. Autobiography of a Labour Party leader. See also (756).
396 Lee, Jennie. *Tomorrow is a new day*. 1942. Autobiographical; in the U.S.A. published as *This great journey* (1942).
397 *Liberal [party] year book*. See (423).
398 Lloyd George, David. *War memoirs of David Lloyd George*. Boston, Mass., 1933—7, 6 vols. Very significant though unreliable.
399 Long, Walter, 1st Viscount Long of Wraxall. *Memories*. New York, n.d. By a Conservative politician; a member of the Cabinet 1895—1905, 1915—21.
400 Low, David. *Years of wrath: a cartoon history 1932—1945*. 1949. Largely reprinted from the London *Evening Standard*.
401 Lucy, Henry. *The diary of a journalist*. 1920—3, 3 vols. On parliament, 1885—1916.
402 Lyttleton, Oliver, Viscount Chandos. *The memoirs of Lord Chandos*. 1962. By an industrialist and a Conservative politician.
403 Macardle, Dorothy. *The Irish Republic: a documented chronicle of the Anglo-Irish conflict and the partitioning of Ireland with a detailed account of the period 1916—1923*. 1937.
404 MacDonald, J. Ramsay. *The socialist movement*. 1911. Cf. companion volumes in Home University Library series: Cecil, Lord Hugh, *Conservatism* [1912], and Hobhouse, Leonard T., *Liberalism*, cited (2326).
405 Macmillan, Harold. *Winds of change 1914—1939*. 1966. *The blast of war 1939—1945*. 1967. *Tides of fortune 1945—1955*. 1969. *Riding the storm 1956—1959*. 1971. *Pointing the way 1959—1961*. 1972. *At the end of the day 1961—1963*. 1973. These volumes of autobiography are revealing as to Macmillan himself; otherwise disappointing.
406 Mann, Tom. *Tom Mann's memoirs*. 1923. Repr., 1967. By a leading trade unionist and communist.
407 Maurice, Nancy (ed.). *The Maurice Case: from the papers of Major-General Sir Frederick Maurice*. [Hamden, Conn.], 1972. Concerns the controversy in May 1918 over Maurice's letter to the press concerning British troop strength.
408 Midleton, William St John F. Brodrick, 1st Earl of. *Records and reactions, 1856—1939*. 1939. Memoirs of a war secretary and secretary for India.
409 Miliband, Ralph and John Saville (eds.). *The socialist register, 1964—*. 1964—. Annual. Analysis of contemporary events, with a long chapter on Britain. Latest volume is for 1973.
410 Minney, Rubeigh J. *The private papers of Hore-Belisha*. 1960.
411 Morgan, Kenneth O. *Lloyd George: family letters 1885—1936*. 1973.
412 Morley, John, Viscount Morley of Blackburn. *Memorandum on resignation, August 1914*. New York, 1928. A classic document.
413 —— *Recollections*. New York, 1917, 2 vols.

414   Morrison, Herbert, Baron Morrison of Lambeth. *Herbert Morrison: an auto-biography*. 1960. Weak on Labour Government of 1945—51.
415   Mosley, Oswald. *My life*. 1968. Tiresome and turgid, but revealing.
416   Newton, Thomas Wodehouse Legh, 2nd Baron. *Retrospection*. 1941. Lord Newton was a diplomat, politician and author.
417   Nicolson, Harold. *Diaries and letters*, ed. Nigel Nicolson. 1966—8, 3 vols. Embraces 1930—62.
418   O'Connor, Thomas P. *Memoirs of an old parliamentarian*. II, New York, 1929. O'Connor was a member of parliament 1885—1929. See also (2453).
419   Pakenham, Francis Aungier, 7th Earl of Longford. *Born to believe: an auto-biography*. 1953. See also his *Five lives* (1964). And his *The grain of wheat* (1974).
420   Pankhurst, Emmeline. *My own story*. 1914. By a militant suffragette.
421   Pankhurst, Christabel. *Unshackled: the story of how we won the vote*, ed. Lord Pethick-Lawrence. 1959. By a daughter of Emmeline Pankhurst.
422   Parmoor, Charles Alfred Cripps, 1st Baron. *A retrospect: looking back over a life of more than eighty years*. 1936. By a Conservative politician who switched to Labour.
423   *Political party year books 1885—1948*. 128 vols. Includes *The constitutional year book, 1885—1939* of the Conservative Party; *The Labour year book, 1895—1948*; *The Liberal yearbook, 1887—1939*; *The Liberal and Radical year book, 1887—1889*. Reprint, Harvester Press, Hassocks, Sussex. Publication concluded, 1974.
424   Pollitt, Harry. *Serving my time: an apprenticeship to politics*. 1940. By a secretary general and chairman of the British Communist Party.
425   Ponsonby, Arthur, Baron. *Falsehood in war-time*. 1928. Documents.
426   Pritt, Denis N. *The autobiography of D.N. Pritt, 1965—66*, 3 vols. Carries Pritt from Toryism to Marxism.
427   *Report of the Royal Commission on the poor laws and the relief of distress*. 1909. Authorized by parliament in 1905.
428   Riddell, George Allardice, Baron. *Lord Riddell's war diary, 1914—1918*. [1923].
429   ——— *More pages from my diary, 1908—1914*. 1934.
430   Robens, Alfred, Baron. *Ten year stint*. 1972. By the chairman of National Coal Board.
431   Rose, Michael E. *The English poor law, 1780—1930*. Newton Abbot, 1971. Documents.
432   Sacks, Benjamin. *J. Ramsay MacDonald in thought and action*. Albuquerque, New Mexico, 1952. Digest of MacDonald's writings and speeches.
433   Salter, James Arthur, 1st Baron. *Memoirs of a public servant*. 1961. See also Salter's *Slave of the lamp: a public servant's notebook*. 1967.
434   Samuel, Herbert Louis, 1st Viscount. *Memoirs*. 1945. Published in the U.S.A. as *Grooves of change: a book of memoirs*. New York, 1946. See also (678).
435   [Shadwell, Arthur]. 'The socialist movement in Great Britain', *The Times*, 7—19 Jan. 1909. An important contemporary statement.
436   Shinwell, Emanuel. *Conflict without malice*. 1955. Autobiographical.
437   Simon, John, Viscount. *Retrospect: the memoirs of the Rt. Hon. Viscount Simon*. 1952. Limited value.
438   Smillie, Robert. *My life for labour*. 1924. By a trade union leader and Labour politician.
439   Snell, Henry, Baron. *Men, movements and myself*. 1936.
440   Snowden, Philip, Viscount. *An autobiography*. 1934, 2 vols.
441   Stevenson, Frances. *The years that are past*. 1967. By Lloyd George's secretary and mistress. See also her *Lloyd George: a diary*, ed. Alan J.P. Taylor. 1971.
442   Swanwick, Helena M.L. *Builders of peace: being ten years' history of the Union of Democratic Control*. 1973. First published in 1924. See also (647).
443   Swinton, Philip Cunliffe-Lister, 1st Earl. *Sixty years of power; some mem-*

17

ories of the men who wielded it. 1966. 'Pictures' of prime ministers from
Balfour to Alec Douglas-Home.
444 Templewood, Samuel Hoare, Viscount. *Nine troubled years.* 1954. Indispensable for 'appeasement' and other matters of state 1931—40.
445 Thomas, James H. *My story.* 1937. Useful for General Strike of 1926.
446 Thorne, Will. *My life's battles.* [1925.] By a trade union official.
447 Tiltman, H. Hessell. *James Ramsay MacDonald: labor's man of destiny.* 1929.
Useful for quotations, writings and speeches — to 1924.
448 Webb, Beatrice. *Beatrice Webb's diaries 1912—1924,* ed. Margaret I. Cole.
1952. Continued by *Beatrice Webb's diaries 1924—1932,* ed. Margaret
Cole. 1956.
449 ——— *Our partnership,* ed. Barbara Drake and Margaret I. Cole. 1948. Autobiography and diaries, 1892—1911.
450 Wedgwood, Josiah C. *Memoirs of a fighting life.* 1941. A Liberal turned
Laborite.
451 Wigg, George, Baron. *George Wigg.* 1972. Autobiography of a Liberal
politician.
452 Williams, Francis. *A prime minister remembers: the war and post-war
memoirs of the Rt. Hon. Earl Attlee.* 1961. Based on interviews;
disappointing.
453 Wilson, Harold. *The Labour government 1964—1970.* 1971. His version.
454 Wilson, Trevor (ed.). *The political diaries of C.P. Scott 1911—1928.* 1970.
455 Winterton, Edward Turnour, 6th Earl. *Fifty tumuluous years.* 1955. Reminiscences of the years 1904—54 by a politician, editor and journalist.
456 Woolton, Frederick James Marquis, Earl of. *Memoirs.* 1959. Woolton was
chairman of the Conservative Party in a crucial period, 1945—51.

2 Surveys
(See also sec. III, above.)

457 Barnett, Correlli. *The collapse of British power.* 1972. A study of the years
1918—40.
458 Boyd, Francis. *British politics in transition 1945—63.* 1964.
459 Buchan, John. *The people's king — George V: a narrative of twenty-five years.*
Boston, 1935. Published in England as *The king's grace.* 1935. Popular
account.
460 Lyons, Francis S.L. *Ireland since the famine.* New York, 1971. Excellent
treatment of the twentieth century.
461 McElwee, William. *Britain's locust years 1918—1940.* 1962.
462 McFarlane, Leslie J. *British politics 1918—64.* 1965.
463 Somervell, David C. *British politics since 1900.* 1950.
464 Thomas, Neville Penry. *A history of British politics from the year 1900.* 1956.

3 Monographs
(See also sec. IV, pt. 3, above.)

465 Agar, Herbert. *Britain alone, June 1940 — June 1941.* 1972. Well-informed
account intended for the general reader.
466 Armitage, Susan. *The politics of decontrol of industry: Britain and the United
States.* 1969. Decontrol after World War I.
467 Bardens, Dennis. *Churchill in parliament.* 1967. Popular; well informed.
468 Barker, Rodney. *Education and politics 1900—1951: a study of the Labour
Party.* 1972.
469 Barry, E. Eldon. *Nationalisation in British politics: the historical background.*
1965.
470 Bassett, Reginald. *Nineteen thirty-one: political crisis.* 1958. Holds that
MacDonald was not disloyal to the Labour Party. See also (304, 859).
471 Bealey, Frank and Henry Pelling. *Labour and politics 1900—1906: a history
of the Labour Representation Committee.* 1958. See also (616).
472 Beaverbrook, William Maxwell Aitken, 1st Baron. *The decline and fall of
Lloyd George.* 1963. On the events of 1921—2.

473   —— *Men and power 1917–1918.* 1956.
474   —— *Politicians and the war 1914–1916.* New York, 1928.
475   Beer, Max. *A history of British socialism*, with an introduction by Richard H. Tawney. 1940.
476   Beer, Samuel H. *British politics in the collectivist age.* New York, 1965.
477   Berrington, Hugh B. *Backbench opinion in the House of Commons, 1945–55.* Oxford, 1973. See also (534).
478   Black, Robert. *Stalinism in Britain.* 1970. Informative but hardly always reliable.
479   Blake, Robert. *The Conservative Party from Peel to Churchill.* New York, 1970. Ford lectures at Oxford in 1968.
480   Blewett, Neal. *The peers, the parties and the people: the General Election of 1910.* 1972. Very detailed.
481   Blumler, Jay G. and Denis McQuail. *Television in politics: its uses and influence.* Chicago, Ill., 1969. The role of television in the General Election, 1964.
482   Bonham, John. *The middle class vote.* 1954. Developments since 1945.
483   Booth, Arthur H. *British hustings 1924–1950.* 1956.
484   Boyce D.G. *Englishmen and Irish troubles: British public opinion and the making of Irish policy 1918–1922.* Cambridge, Mass., 1972.
485   Brady, Robert A. *Crisis in Britain: plans and achievements of the Labour Government.* 1950. Examination of 'middle-way Socialism' after World War II.
486   Brand, Carl F. *The British Labour Party: a short history.* Rev. ed., Stanford, Cal., 1973. Brief narrative; excellent for reference.
487   —— *British labour's rise to power: eight studies.* 1941. Includes significant essays on 1914–18.
488   Brown, R. Douglas. *The battle of Crichel Down.* 1955. Concerns parliamentary dispute over sale of government land in Dorset.
489   Butler, David and Donald Stokes. *Political change in Britain: forces shaping electoral choice.* 1969. Study of recent electoral trends.
490   Butler, David E. *The electoral system in Britain since 1918.* 2nd ed., Oxford, 1963.
491   —— *British General Election of 1951.* 1952.
492   —— *British General Election of 1955.* 1955.
493   —— and Richard Rose. *The British General Election of 1959.* 1960.
494   —— and Anthony King. *The British General Election of 1964.* 1965.
495   —— and Anthony King. *The British General Election of 1966.* 1966.
496   —— and Michael Pinto-Duschinsky. *The British General Election of 1970.* 1971.
497   Butt, Ronald. *The power of parliament.* 1967. Assesses role of parliament in politics, 1945–67.
498   Canning, John (ed.). *Living history: 1914.* 1968. A symposium; well done.
499   Carberry, Thomas F. *Consumers in politics: a history and general review of the Co-operative Party.* Manchester, 1969. Based on careful research.
500   Carpenter, Niles. *Guild Socialism.* New York, 1922. Rather slight.
501   'Cato' [pseud.]. *Guilty men.* 1940. Indictment of appeasement.
502   Chester, Lewis *et al. The Zinoviev letter.* Philadelphia, 1968.
503   Churchill, Randolph S. *The fight for the Tory leadership.* Boston, 1964. Conservative politics 1957–63; hardly definitive.
504   —— *The rise and fall of Sir Anthony Eden.* New York, 1959. Good interim study.
505   Clarke, Peter F. *Lancashire and the new Liberalism.* Cambridge, 1971. Develops the thesis that World War I destroyed the Liberal Party.
506   Cline, Catherine Ann. *Recruits to Labour; the British Labour Party, 1914–1931.* Syracuse, N.Y., 1963.
507   Coffey, Thomas M. *Agony at Easter: the 1916 uprising.* New York, 1969.
508   Cole, George D.H. *History of the Labour Party from 1914.* 1948. The best account; includes detailed list of party programmes, reports, pamphlets, 1914–47.
509   Cole, Margaret. *The story of Fabian socialism.* 1961. Informative.

POLITICAL HISTORY

510 —— (ed.). *The Webbs and their work*. 1949. Critical analysis.
511 Colvin, Ian. *The Chamberlain Cabinet*. 1971. Based on Cabinet papers.
512 Cook, Chris and John Ramsden (eds.). *By-elections in British politics*. 1973. A study by periods; twelve essays by various writers.
513 Cowling, Maurice. *The impact of Labour, 1920—24: the beginning of modern British politics*. Cambridge, 1970. First detailed study of these years.
514 Craton, Michael and Herbert W. McCready. *The great Liberal revival, 1903—6*. 1966. Brief, but useful for polling.
515 Crick, Bernard (ed.). *Essays on reform 1967*. 1967.
516 Crosby, Gerda Richards. *Disarmament and peace in British politics 1914—1919*. 1957.
517 Cross, Colin. *The Fascists in Britain*. 1961. Still useful but see (191).
518 —— *The Liberals in power (1905—1914)*. 1963. Aims to be both 'comprehensive' and 'brief'.
519 Crossman, Richard H.S. (ed.). *New Fabian essays*. 1952. By various writers; to be compared with original *Fabian essays* (1889).
520 Dangerfield, George. *The strange death of Liberal England*. New York, 1935. Brilliant, and stimulating, but frequently unreliable.
521 Das, Manmath N. *India under Morley and Minto: politics behind revolution, repression and reforms*. 1964. Based on Morley and Minto papers.
522 Dennis, Peter. *Decision by default: peacetime conscription and British defence, 1919—1939*. 1972.
523 Donaldson, Frances. *The Marconi scandal*. 1962. Finally, a reliable account.
524 Dorfman, Gerald A. *Wage politics in Britain 1945—67; Government vs. the TUC*. Ames, Iowa, 1973.
525 Douglas, Roy. *The history of the Liberal Party 1895—1970*. 1971. Disappointing; valuable only for party organization.
526 Dowse, Robert E. *Left in the centre: the Independent Labour Party 1893—1940*. 1966. Sympathetic treatment of decline of the I.L.P. after 1918.
527 Driver, Christopher. *The disarmers: a study in protest*. 1964. Especially the CND movement and left wing revolt from Labour policy.
528 Eade, Charles (ed.). *Churchill by his contemporaries*. 1953. Forty essays by different authors.
529 Eckstein, Harry. *Pressure group politics: the case of the British Medical Association*. Stanford, Cal., 1960.
530 Einzig, Paul. *Decline and fall? Britain's crisis in the sixties*. 1969.
531 Emy, H.V. *Liberals, radicals and social politics 1892—1914*. Cambridge, 1973. Adds detail based on manuscript collections.
532 Fergusson, James. *The Curragh incident*. 1964. The best treatment.
533 Finer, Samuel E. *Anonymous empire: a study of the lobby in Great Britain*. 2nd ed., 1966. Based on examples, 1962—5.
534 Finer, Samuel E. and Hugh B. Berrington and David J. Bartholomew. *Backbench opinion in the House of Commons 1955—59*. Oxford, 1961. On matters of defence. See also (477).
535 Foot, Paul. *The politics of Harold Wilson*. 1968. Informative but polemical.
536 Fraser, Derek. *The evolution of the British welfare state: a history of social policy since the Industrial Revolution*. 1973. Extensive treatment of twentieth century.
537 Fulford, Roger. *Votes for women*. 1957. Clear narrative, hardly adequate.
538 Gainer, Bernard. *The alien invasion: the origins of the Aliens Act of 1905*. Ithaca, N.Y., 1972.
539 Gilbert, Bentley B. *British social policy 1914—1939*. Ithaca, N.Y., 1970.
540 —— *The evolution of national insurance in Great Britain: the origins of the welfare state*. 1966. First comprehensive study.
541 Goldsworthy, David. *Colonial issues in British politics, 1945—1961*. Oxford, 1971.
542 Gollin, Alfred M. *Balfour's burden: Arthur Balfour and imperial preference*. 1965.
543 Gordon-Walker, Patrick. *The Cabinet: political authority in Britain*. New York, 1970.

544 Grainger, John H. *Character and style in English politics*. Cambridge, 1969. Interesting inquiry.

545 Granzow, Brigitte. *A mirror of Nazism: British opinion and the emergence of Hitler, 1929—1933*. 1964.

546 Graubard, Stephen. *British labour and the Russian revolution, 1917—1924*. 1956.

547 Gregory, Roy. *The miners and British politics, 1906—1914*. Oxford, 1968.

548 Gretton, Peter. *Former naval person: Winston Churchill and the royal navy*. 1968.

549 Guinn, Paul. *British strategy and politics, 1914 to 1918*. Oxford, 1965. Relations between generals and politicians.

550 Gwynn, Denis. *The history of partition (1912—1925)*. Dublin, 1950. As good a general account as we have.

551 Hadley, W.H. *Munich: before and after*. 1944. Analysis of newspaper coverage.

552 Halévy, Elie. *A history of the English people in the nineteenth century*, V, *Imperialism and the rise of labour*; VI, *The rule of democracy 1905—1914*, tr. Edward Ingram Watkin. 2nd ed., 1951—3. This celebrated work of a noted French scholar stands up well despite revision of much of his interpretation.

553 Hankey, Maurice P.A., 1st Baron. *The supreme command, 1914—1918*. 1961, 2 vols. By the secretary of the War Cabinet.

554 —— *Government control in war*. Cambridge, 1945. Knowles Lectures, Cambridge, 1945.

555 Hanson, Albert H. *Parliament and public ownership*. 1961.

556 Harrison, Martin. *Trade unions and the Labour Party since 1945*. 1960. Dispassionate treatment.

557 Haseler, Stephen. *The Gaitskellites: revisionism in the British Labour Party 1951—64*. 1969. Thorough.

558 Hazlehurst, Cameron. *Politicians at war, July 1914 to May 1915*. 1971. To be continued.

559 Hicks, Ursula K. *The finance of British government 1920—1936*. 1938. Much more detail than (231).

560 Hindess, Barry. *The decline of working-class politics*. 1971. Examination of the period 1950—70. See also (792).

561 Hinton, James. *The first shop stewards' movement*. 1974. During World War I. See also (617).

562 Hodder-Williams, Richard. *Public opinion polls and British politics*. 1970.

563 Hoffman, John D. *Conservative Party in opposition, 1945—51*. 1964.

564 Hohman, Helen Fisher. *The development of social insurance and minimum wage legislation in Great Britain*. Boston, Mass., 1933.

565 Hope, James F. *A history of the 1900 parliament*. 1908. On 1900—1.

566 Hyam, Ronald R. *Elgin and Churchill at the Colonial Office*. 1905—8. New York, 1968. Gives Elgin his due.

567 [Illingworth, Percy H.] . *The government record 1906—1913: seven years of Liberal legislation and administration*. 1913. Detailed account by Liberal Party Publication Department.

568 Irving, Clive *et al. Scandal '63; a study of the Profumo affair*. 1963.

569 Jackson, Robert J. *Rebels and whips: an analysis of dissension, discipline and cohesion in British political parties*. 1968. Analysis of period 1945—64.

570 James, Robert Rhodes. *Ambitions and realities: British politics 1964—1970*. 1972.

571 Janosik, Edward G. *Constituency Labour Parties in Britain*. 1968. Based on 1964 General Election.

572 Jenkins, Peter. *The battle of Downing Street*. 1970. The 'political crisis' of June 1969. Instant history, but stimulating.

573 [Johnson, Francis] . *The I.L.P. in war and peace: a short account of the Party from its foundation to the present day*. 1942.

574 Johnson, Paul Barton. *Land fit for heroes: the planning of British reconstruction*. Chicago, Ill., 1968. An important book.

575 Judd, Denis. *Balfour and the British Empire: a study in imperial evolution 1874—1932.* 1968.

576 Kellas, James G. *The Scottish political system.* Cambridge, 1973. Includes recent political history.

577 Kendall, Walter. *The revolutionary movement in Britain 1900—1921: the origins of British communism.* 1969.

578 Kinnear, Michael. *The British voter: an atlas and survey since 1885.* Ithaca, N.Y., 1968. 'A study of the economic and social background of politics'; goes through the General Election of 1966.

579 —— *The fall of Lloyd George: the political crisis of 1922.* 1973.

580 Klugmann, James. *History of the Communist Party of Great Britain.* 1969, 2 vols. Strongly partisan. Cf. (593, 611).

581 Koss, Stephen E. *John Morley at the India Office, 1905—1910.* 1969.

582 —— *Lord Haldane, scapegoat for Liberalism.* New York, 1969. A controversial contribution to the political crisis of May 1915. Cf. (558).

583 Lapping, Brian. *The Labour Government, 1964—70.* 1970. Instant history.

584 Le May, Godfrey H.L. *British supremacy in South Africa 1899—1907.* Oxford, 1965.

585 Levin, Bernard. *The pendulum years: Britain and the sixties.* 1970. A wide examination.

586 Lewis, Ben W. *British planning and nationalization.* New York, 1952. Detailed account of developments 1945—51.

587 Livingstone, Adelaide and Marjorie Scott Johnson. *The Peace Ballot: the official history.* 1935. Prepared by the National Declaration Committee.

588 Lyman, Richard. *The first Labour government, 1924.* [1957].

589 McCallum, Ronald B. *Public opinion and the last peace.* 1944. On the Versailles settlement.

590 —— and Alison Readman. *The British General Election of 1945.* 1947.

591 McCarran, M. Margaret Patricia. *Fabianism in the political life of Britain 1919—1931.* 2nd ed., Chicago, 1954. The most complete account for these years but sometimes misleading.

592 Maccoby, Simon. *English radicalism: the end?* 1961. Concerns 1906—31.

593 MacFarlane, Leslie J. *The British Communist Party; its origin and development until 1929.* 1966. A favourable account intelligently presented. Cf. (580).

594 McHenry, Dean E. *His Majesty's Opposition: structure and problems of the British Labour Party, 1931—1938.* Berkeley, Cal., 1940.

595 McKenzie, Robert T. *British political parties; the distribution of power within the Conservative and Labour parties.* 2nd ed., 1963.

596 McKenzie, Robert T. and Allan Silver. *Angels in marble: working class conservatives in urban England.* 1968.

597 McKie, David and Chris Cook (eds.). *The decade of disillusion: British politics in the sixties.* 1972. Essays by various writers.

598 Matthew, Henry C.G. *The Liberal Imperialists: the ideas and politics of a post-Gladstonian élite.* 1973. Unfortunately, largely restricted to the leadership.

599 Mendelssohn, Peter de. *The age of Churchill: heritage and adventure 1874—1911.* 1961. Popular; somewhat marred by errors.

600 Middlemas, Robert Keith. *The Clydesiders: a left wing struggle for parliamentary power.* 1965. The role of Glasgow Independent Labour Party members of parliament 1922—31.

601 Miliband, Ralph. *Parliamentary socialism: a study in the politics of labour.* 1961. A general view since 1906.

602 Morgan, Kenneth O. *The age of Lloyd George.* 1971. Its survey of 'the revival, triumph, division and decline' of the Liberal Party is the best brief discussion. Accompanied with documents.

603 Morris, Andrew J. Anthony. *Radicalism against war 1906—1914.* Totowa, N.J., 1972. Especially as reflected in parliament and in the press.

604 Nicholas, Herbert G. *The British General Election of 1950.* 1951.

605 Nordlinger, Eric. *The working-class Tories.* Berkeley, Cal., 1967.

606 Ó Broin, Léon. *The chief secretary: Augustine Birrell in Ireland.* 1969.

607   O'Leary, Cornelius. *The elimination of corrupt practices in British elections, 1868–1911.* 1962.
608   Pakenham, Francis Aungier, 7th Earl of Longford. *Peace by ordeal: an account from first-hand sources of the negotiation and signature of the Anglo-Irish Treaty, 1921.* 1935.
609   Parkinson, Roger. *Blood, toil, tears and sweat: the war history from Dunkirk to Alamein, based on the War Cabinet papers of 1940 to 1942.* 1973. Continued by his *A day's march nearer home: the war history from Alamein to VE Day based on the War Cabinet papers of 1942 to 1945.* New York, 1974.
610   Pease, Edward R. *The history of the Fabian Society.* 2nd ed., 1925.
611   Pelling, Henry. *The British Communist Party: a historical profile.* 1958. Reliable. See also (593).
612   —— *Popular politics and society in late Victorian Britain: essays.* 1968. Includes significant essays relative to the twentieth century.
613   —— *A short history of the Labour Party.* 1961. Interesting judgments.
614   Petrie, Charles. *The Carlton Club.* 1955.
615   Plowden, William. *The motor car and politics 1896–1970.* 1971. Well researched and well argued.
616   Poirier, Philip P. *The advent of the British Labour Party.* 1958. See also (471).
617   Pribićević, Branko. *The shop stewards' movement and workers' control 1910–1922.* Oxford, 1959. See also (561).
618   Pritt, Denis N. *The Labour Government 1945–51.* 1963. Hostile account.
619   Pulzer, Peter G.J. *Political representation and elections: parties and voting in Great Britain.* 1967. On the period 1945–66.
620   Punnett, Robert M. *Front-bench opposition: the role of the leader of the Opposition, the shadow Cabinet and shadow Government in British politics.* 1973. Principally in 1951–70 period. See also (655).
621   Rae, John. *Conscience and politics: the British government and the conscientious objector to military service 1916–1919.* 1970. Cf. Boulton, David. *Objection overruled.* 1967.
622   Rasmussen, Jorgen Scott. *The Liberal Party: a study of retrenchment and revival.* [1965]. In the United States published as: *Retrenchment and revival: a study of the contemporary British Liberal Party.* Tucson, Ariz. [1964]. On developments since 1945.
623   Raymond, John (ed.). *The Baldwin Age.* 1960. Interesting, useful essays on political, economic and cultural themes by various authors.
624   Rees, Goronwy. *A chapter of accidents.* 1972. Mainly concerning Guy Burgess and Donald Maclean.
625   Rempel, Richard A. *Unionists divided: Arthur Balfour, Joseph Chamberlain and the Unionist free traders.* 1972.
626   Richards, Peter G. *Honourable members: a study of the British backbencher.* 1959.
627   —— *Parliament and conscience.* 1970. Discussion of issues in Private Member Bills dealing with capital punishment, homosexuality, divorce, abortion, Sunday entertainment, and censorship in the theatre.
628   —— *Patronage in the British government.* 1963.
629   Richter, Irving. *Political purpose in trade unions.* 1973. Concerns period 1950–70.
630   Robson, William A. (ed.). *'The Political Quarterly' in the thirties.* 1971. Articles by Bishop Henson, G.D.H. Cole, R.H. Tawney, Bertrand Russell, Leonard Woolf, *et al.* Valuable introduction.
631   Rogow, Arnold A. *The Labour Government and British industry, 1945–1951.* Oxford, 1955.
632   Rosecrance, R.N. *Defense of the realm: British strategy in the nuclear epoch.* New York, 1968. Concerns the period 1946–57. For more comprehensive treatment see Pierre, Andrew J. *Nuclear politics: the British experience with an independent strategic force, 1939–1970.* 1972.
633   Rowland, Peter. *The last Liberal governments: the promised land, 1905–1910.* 1968.
634   —— *The last Liberal governments: unfinished business, 1911–1914.* 1971.

This and (633) provide the most comprehensive account of politics, 1905—14.

635   Russell, A.K. *Liberal landslide: the General Election of 1906*. 1973.

636   Scanlon, John. *Decline and fall of the Labour Party*. [1932]. Especially the events of 1931; a contemporary account from Clydeside point of view.

637   Schoenfeld, Maxwell Philip. *The war ministry of Winston Churchill*. Ames, Iowa, 1972.

638   Searle, Geoffrey R. *The quest for national efficiency: a study in British politics and political thought 1899—1914*. Berkeley, Cal. 1971.

639   Sherman, Ari J. *Britain and refugees from the Third Reich, 1933—1939*. 1974.

640   Shrimsley, Anthony. *The first hundred days of Harold Wilson*. New York, 1965. Interesting instant history.

641   Skidelsky, Robert. *Politicians and the slump: the Labour Government of 1929—1931*. 1967.

642   Snyder, William P. *The politics of British defense policy, 1945—1962*. [Columbus, Ohio]. 1964.

643   Southgate, Donald (ed.). *The Conservative leadership 1832—1932*. 1974.

644   Stacey, Frank. *The British ombudsman*. Oxford, 1971.

645   Stewart, Anthony T.Q. *The Ulster crisis*. 1967. Excellent on the crisis of 1911—14.

646   Stuart, Campbell. *Secrets of Crewe house: the story of a famous campaign*. 1920. An account of Northcliffe's Department of Foreign Propaganda in Foreign Countries, organized February 1918.

647   Swartz, Marvin. *The Union of Democratic Control in British politics during the First World War*. Oxford, 1971. Largely from manuscript sources.

648   Taylor, Alan J.P. *et al. Churchill revised: a critical assessment*. New York, 1969. Churchill considered as statesman, politician, historian, military strategist and 'the man'.

649   Taylor, Alan J.P. (ed.). *Lloyd George: twelve essays*. New York, 1971. Results of research stimulated by the Lloyd George Papers at the Beaverbrook Library.

650   Thompson, Laurence Victor. *1940*. New York, 1966. Readable narrative.

651   Thomson, George Malcolm. *The twelve days: 24 July to 4 August 1914*. 1964. An account of British policy and opinion.

652   Townsend, Peter and Nicholas Bosanquet. *Labour and inequality: a study in social policy 1964—70*. 1972.

653   Tracey, Herbert (ed.). *The book of the Labour Party: its history, growth, policy and leaders*. [1925], 3 vols.

654   Trask, David F. *Captains and Cabinets: Anglo-American naval relations, 1917—1918*. Columbia, Mo., 1972.

655   Turner, D.R. *The shadow Cabinet in British politics*. 1969. During the nineteenth and twentieth centuries. See also (620).

656   Watkins, Alan, *The Liberal dilemma*. 1966. 'Primarily a study of the party in its external relations' since 1945.

657   Watkins, Ernest. *The cautious revolution: Britain today and tomorrow*. New York, 1950. Surveys the period 1945—50.

658   Watkins, K.W. *Britain divided: the effect of the Spanish Civil War on British public opinion*. 1963.

659   Wheeler-Bennett, John (ed.). *Action this day: working with Churchill*. 1968. Comment by six men who served Churchill.

660   Williams, Desmond (ed.). *The Irish struggle 1916—1926*. 1966. Fifteen scholarly essays by various authors.

661   Willis, Irene Cooper. *England's holy war: a study of English liberal idealism during the great war*. New York, 1928. In England published in three volumes: *How we went to war*. 1919. *How we got on with the war*. 1920. *How we came out of the war*. 1921.

662   Wilson, Arnold. *Old age pensions: a historical and critical study*. 1941.

663   Wilson, Trevor. *The downfall of the Liberal Party, 1914—1935*. Ithaca, N.Y., 1966. Concludes that developments during World War I were mainly responsible.

664 Winter, J.M. *Socialism and the challenge of war: ideas and politics in Britain 1912—18.* 1974.
665 Wolpert, Stanley A. *Morley and India. 1906—1910.* Berkeley, Cal., 1967.
666 Wootton, Graham. *The politics of influence: British ex-servicemen, Cabinet decisions and cultural change (1917—57).* 1963.
667 Younger, Calton. *Ireland's civil war.* 1968. Especially 1920—3; uses Cabinet Papers.

4 Biographies
(see also sec. IV, pt. 4, above.)

668 Adam, Colin Forbes. *Life of Lord Lloyd.* 1948.
669 Adams, William S. *Edwardian portraits.* 1957. Concerning Edward VII, W.S. Blunt, Sir Robert Baden-Powell, Lord Leverhulme and E.D. Morel.
670 Allen, Bernard M. *Sir Robert Morant: a great public servant.* 1934.
671 Amery, Julian. *The life of Joseph Chamberlain,* IV—VI. 1951—69. Completes J.L. Garvin. *The life of Joseph Chamberlain,* I—III. 1932—4. See also Fraser, Peter. *Joseph Chamberlain: radicalism and empire, 1868—1914.* 1966.
672 Baldwin, Arthur W. *Baldwin, my father; the true story.* 1956. An answer to (783).
673 Birkenhead, Frederick W.F. Smith, 2nd Earl of. *F.E.: the life of F.E. Smith, First Earl of Birkenhead.* 1959.
674 —— *Halifax: the life of Lord Halifax.* 1965. The best biography.
675 Blake, Robert. *The unknown prime minister: the life and times of Andrew Bonar Law 1858—1923.* 1955. One of the very best political biographies.
676 Blaxland, Gregory. *J.H. Thomas: a life for unity.* 1964. Apologetic and unconvincing. See also (445).
677 Bonham Carter, Violet. *Winston Churchill as I knew him.* 1965. Published in the United States as *Winston Churchill — an intimate portrait.* New York, 1965.
678 Bowle, John. *Viscount Samuel: a biography.* 1957. See also (434).
679 Brittain, Vera. *Pethick Lawrence — a portrait.* 1963. Concerning the Labour politician, Frederick William Pethick-Lawrence.
680 Brockway, A. Fenner. *Socialism over sixty years: the life of Jowett of Bradford (1864—1944).* 1946.
681 Brodrick, Alan Houghton. *Near to greatness: a life of the sixth Earl Winterton.* 1965.
682 Bullock, Alan. *The life and times of Ernest Bevin.* 1960—7, 2 vols. In progress, thus far to 1945; one of the best biographies of a public figure.
683 Butler, James R.M. *Lord Lothian (Philip Kerr) 1882—1940.* 1960. Information on the Round Table Group.
684 Churchill, Randolph S. *Lord Derby, 'King of Lancashire': the official life of Edward, 17th Earl of Derby, 1865—1948.* 1959.
685 Churchill, Randolph S. and Martin Gilbert. *Winston S. Churchill.* New York, 1966—71, 3 vols. Presently to 1916; in progress; the official life. See (349) for accompanying documents.
686 Churchill, Winston S. *Great contemporaries.* New York, 1937. Essays written 1929—37; include George V, Rosebery, Shaw, Joseph Chamberlain, John Morley, Asquith and Curzon.
687 Cocks, F. Seymour. *E.D. Morel, the man and his work.* 1920. Inadequate; Dr Catherine Ann Cline has in progress a new biography.
688 Cole, Margaret. *Beatrice Webb.* New York, 1946.
689 —— *Makers of the labour movement.* 1948. Biographical sketches including Blatchford, Hardie, S. Webb, Arthur Henderson, George Lansbury and H.G. Wells.
690 Cooke, Colin. *The life of Richard Stafford Cripps.* 1957. 'Official' life.
691 Crewe, Robert O.A. Crewe-Milnes, 1st Marquis. *Lord Rosebery.* 1931. See also (722).
692 Cross, Colin. *Philip Snowden.* 1966.
693 de Bunsen, Victoria A. *Charles Roden Buxton; a memoir.* 1948.

694   Dickie, John. *The uncommon commoner: a study of Sir Alec Douglas-Home*. 1964.

695   Donoughue, Bernard and G.W. Jones. *Herbert Morrison: portrait of a politician*. 1973. 'Official', sympathetic, thorough.

696   Driberg, Tom. *Beaverbrook: a study in power and frustration*. 1956. Cf. (772).

697   Dugdale, Blanche E.C. *Arthur James Balfour, First Earl of Balfour*. 1936, 2 vols. For many years the standard; now cf. (784, 786).

698   Elton, Godfrey, Baron. *The life of James Ramsay MacDonald (1866—1919)*. 1939.

699   Ervine, St John G. *Craigavon, Ulsterman*. 1949. Life of James Craig.

700   Feiling, Keith. *The life of Neville Chamberlain*. 1946. Still the best biography.

701   Fisher, Herbert A.L. *James Bryce (Viscount Bryce of Dechmont, O.M.)*. New York, 1927, 2 vols.

702   Fisher, Nigel. *Iain Macleod*. 1973.

703   Foot, Michael. *Aneurin Bevan: a biography*. 1962—73, 2 vols. Supersedes Vincent Brome, *Aneurin Bevan*. 1953.

704   Fraser, Peter. *Lord Esher: a political biography*. 1973. See also (367).

705   Gooch, George P. *Life of Lord Courtney*. 1920.

706   Grigg, John. *The young Lloyd George*. 1973. Uses new material; through the Boer War.

707   Gwynn, Denis. *The Life of John Redmond*. 1932.

708   Halpérin, Vladimir. *Lord Milner and the empire: the evolution of British imperialism*. [1952].

709   Hamer, David A. *John Morley: Liberal intellectual in politics*. Oxford, 1968.

710   Hamilton, Mary Agnes. *Arthur Henderson: a biography*. 1938.

711   —— *Sidney and Beatrice Webb: a study in contemporary biography*. 1933.

712   Hancock, William Keith. *Smuts: the Sanguine years, 1870—1919*. 1962. *Smuts: the fields of force, 1919—1950*. 1968. (see 380).

713   Hughes, Emrys. *Keir Hardie*. 1956. Inadequate as are earlier biographies.

714   —— *Sydney Silverman, rebel in parliament*. 1969.

715   Hutchinson, George. *Edward Heath*. 1970. Journalistic; informative. Cf. Laing, Margaret. *Edward Heath, prime minister*. 1972.

716   Hyde, H. Montgomery. *Baldwin: the unexpected prime minister*. 1973. The latest full length treatment.

717   —— *Carson, the life of Sir Edward Carson, Lord Carson of Duncairn*. 1953. Hyde uses sources not available to Marjoribanks and Colvin (739).

718   —— *Lord Reading: the life of Rufus Isaacs. First Marquess of Reading*. 1967.

719   Inglis, Brian. *Roger Casement*. New York, 1973. The best study.

720   Isaacs, Gerald Rufus, 2nd Marquess of Reading. *Rufus Isaacs, First Marquess of Reading, 1860—1914*. 1942—5, 2 vols.

721   James, Robert Rhodes. *Churchill: a study in failure 1900—1939*. 1970. Useful for period 1918—39.

722   —— *Rosebery: a biography of Archibald Philip, fifth earl of Rosebery*. 1963. Replaces (691) as standard.

723   Jenkins, Roy H. *Asquith: portrait of a man and an era*. 1964. The best biography.

724   —— *Mr Attlee: an interim biography*. 1948. Still informative.

725   Johnson, Alan Campbell. *Sir Anthony Eden: a biography*. Rev. ed., 1955.

726   Jones, Thomas. *Lloyd George*. Cambridge, Mass., 1951. Slight before 1914; thereafter about as good as there is.

727   Kent, William. *John Burns: labour's lost leader*. 1950. A more adequate biography is badly needed.

728   Koss, Stephen E. *Sir John Brunner: radical plutocrat 1842—1919*. Cambridge, 1970. Brunner was an industrialist; also president of the National Liberal Federation, 1911—18.

729   Larkin, Emmet. *James Larkin: Irish labour leader, 1876—1947*. Cambridge, Mass., 1965.

730   Lloyd George, Richard, 2nd Earl. *Lloyd George*. 1960.

731 Lyons, Francis S.L. *John Dillon: a biography.* 1968. Dillon was an Irish Nationalist politician.
732 McDermott, Geoffrey. *Leader lost: a biography of Hugh Gaitskell.* 1972. Informative.
733 Mackail, John W. and Guy Wyndham. *Life and letters of George Wyndham.* n.d., 2 vols. Wyndham was a statesman and man of letters.
734 McKenna, Stephen. *Reginald McKenna 1863–1943, a memoir.* 1948.
735 MacLeod, Iain. *Neville Chamberlain.* 1961. But see (700).
736 McNair, John. *James Maxton, the beloved rebel.* 1955.
737 Magnus, Philip. *Kitchener: portrait of an imperialist.* 1958. The most recent and the best biography.
738 Mallet, Charles. *Herbert Gladstone: a memoir.* 1932.
739 Marjoribanks, Edward and Ian Colvin. *The Life of Lord Carson.* 1932–6, 3 vols. See also (717).
740 Martin, Kingsley. *Harold Laski (1893–1950): a biographical memoir.* 1953.
741 Marwick, Arthur J.B. *Clifford Allen: the open conspirator.* 1964.
742 Masterman, Lucy. *C.F.G. Masterman: a biography.* 1939. Includes diary entries and much correspondence.
743 Maurice, Frederick. *Haldane, 1858–1928: the life of Viscount Haldane of Cloan.* 1929, 2 vols. See also (766).
744 Middlemas, Keith and John Barnes. *Baldwin: a biography.* 1969. Cf. Barbara C. Malament, 'Baldwin re-stored?', *JMH*, 44 (Mar. 1972), 87–96. See also (716).
745 Minney, Rubeigh J. *Viscount Addison: leader of the Lords.* 1946.
746 Moran, Charles McMoran Wilson, Baron. *Churchill: taken from the diaries of Lord Moran: the struggle for survival, 1940–1965.* Boston, Mass., 1966.
747 Murphy, J.T. [John Thomas]. *Labour's big three: a biographical study of Clement Attlee, Herbert Morrison and Ernest Bevin.* 1953. A popular treatment.
748 Murray, Arthur C. *Master and brother: Murrays of Elibank.* 1945.
749 Newton, Thomas Wodehouse Legh, 2nd Baron. *Lord Lansdowne: a biography.* 1929.
750 Owen, Frank. *Tempestuous journey: Lloyd George, his life and times.* 1954. Interesting material but a book disappointing in its ideas and conclusions.
751 Pakenham, Francis Aungier, 7th Earl of Longford and Thomas P. O'Neill. *Eamon de Valera.* 1970.
752 Pelling, Henry. *Churchill.* 1974. Much more analytical than (685); the best complete life.
753 Petrie, Charles. *The life and letters of Sir Austen Chamberlain.* 1939–40, 2 vols.
754 ——— *Walter Long and his times.* 1936.
755 Pope-Hennessy, James. *Lord Crewe, 1858–1945, the likeness of a Liberal.* 1955.
756 Postgate, Raymond W. *The life of George Lansbury.* 1951. See also (395).
757 Pound, Reginald and Geoffrey Harmsworth. *Northcliffe.* 1959.
758 [Rhondda, Viscountess.] *The life of D.A. Thomas, by his daughter and others.* 1921.
759 Rodgers, W.T. (ed.). *Hugh Gaitskell, 1906–1963.* 1964. Twelve essays.
760 Ronaldshay, Lawrence John Lumley Dundas, Earl of. *The life of Lord Curzon.* [1928], 3 vols. The 'official biography' and still the only complete life; inadequate.
761 Roskill, Stephen W. *Hankey: man of secrets.* 1970–4, 3 vols. Authorized biography, based on Hankey's diary and other papers.
762 Roth, Andrew. *Enoch Powell: tory tribune.* 1970.
763 Salvidge, Stanley. *Salvidge of Liverpool: behind the political scenes, 1890–1928.* 1934.
764 Sampson, Anthony. *Macmillan, a study in ambiguity.* 1967. An assessment.
765 Smith, Janet Adam. *John Buchan; a biography.* 1965. See also (342).
766 Sommer, Dudley. *Haldane of Cloan, his life and times 1856–1928.* 1960. Weak on Haldane at the War Office, but generally more adequate than (743).

767 Spender, John A. and Cyril Asquith. *Life of Herbert Henry Asquith, Lord Oxford and Asquith.* 1932, 2 vols. But see (723).
768 Spender, John A. *The life of the Right Hon. Sir Henry Campbell-Bannerman, G.C.B.* Boston, Mass., 1924, 2 vols. For many years the standard work, now in many ways superseded by (781).
769 Spender, John A. *Sir Robert Hudson, a memoir.* 1930.
770 Stansky, Peter (ed.). *Churchill: a profile.* 1973. Reprints essays, some 'admiring' and some 'critical'.
771 Sykes, Christopher. *Nancy: the life of Lady Astor.* New York, 1972. Supersedes Collis, Maurice. *Nancy Astor.* 1960.
772 Taylor, Alan J.P. *Beaverbrook.* 1972. Extraordinarily fascinating and provocative.
773 Thomas, Hugh. *John Strachey.* 1973. Based on Strachey's papers, but disappointing.
774 Thompson, Laurence Victor. *The enthusiasts: a biography of John and Katharine Bruce Glasier.* 1971. Largely from original sources.
775 Thomson, Malcolm. *David Lloyd George: the official biography.* 1948.
776 Trevelyan, George Macaulay. *Grey of Falloden: the life and letters of Sir Edward Grey, afterwards Viscount Grey of Falloden.* Boston, Mass., 1937. Still of great interest though in scholarship superseded by (1102).
777 Waley, S.D. *Edwin Montagu.* 1964. Montagu was secretary of state for India, 1917—22.
778 Wedgwood, C. Veronica. *The last of the Radicals: Josiah Wedgwood, M.P.* 1951.
779 Weir, L. MacNeill. *The tragedy of Ramsay MacDonald: a political biography.* 1938. Very little after 1931.
780 Wheeler-Bennett, John W. *John Anderson, Viscount Waverly.* 1962.
781 Wilson, John. *CB: a life of Sir Henry Campbell-Bannerman.* 1973. More scholarly detail than (768) but interpretation not much modified.
782 Wrench, John Evelyn. *Alfred Lord Milner; the man of no illusions 1854—1925.* 1958.
783 Young, George M. *Stanley Baldwin.* 1952. One of the great disappointments of historical scholarship.
784 Young, Kenneth. *Arthur James Balfour: the happy life of the politician, prime minister, statesman and philosopher 1848—1930.* 1963. Much better than (697).
785 —— *Churchill and Beaverbrook: a study in friendship and politics.* 1966. Narrative treatment of 1910—65 based largely on the Beaverbrook papers.
786 Zebel, Sydney H. *Balfour: a political biography.* Cambridge, 1973. Excellent.

5 Articles
(See also sec. IV, pt. 5, above.)

787 Abrams, Philip and Alan Little. 'The young voter in British politics', *BJS*, XVI (June 1965), 95—110.
788 Anderson, Alan. 'The labour laws and the Cabinet Legislative Committee of 1926—27', *Bulletin, Society for the Study of Labour History*, XXIII (Autumn 1971), 37—54.
789 Barker, Bernard. 'Anatomy of reformism: the social and political ideas of the labour leadership in Yorkshire', *IRSH*, XVIII (pt. 1, 1973), 1—27.
790 Barker, Rodney. 'The Labour Party and education for socialism', *IRSH*, XIV (pt. 1, 1969), 22—53.
791 Bassett, Reginald. 'Telling the truth to the people: the myth of the Baldwin "Confession" ', *Cambridge Journal*, II (Nov. 1948), 84—95.
792 Baxter, R. 'The working class and labour politics', *PS*, XX (no. 1, 1972), 97—107.
793 Beer, Samuel H. 'The representation of interests in the British government: historical background', *American Political Science Review*, LI (Sept. 1957), 613—50.
794 Benewick, R.J. *et al.* 'The floating voter and the Liberal view of represen-

tation', *PS*, XVII (1969), 177—95. Examination of voting behaviour and political opinion, 1950—62.

795 Bisceglia, Louis R. 'Norman Angell and the "pacifist" muddle', *BIHR*, XLV (May 1972), 104—21.

796 Blewett, Neal. 'Free fooders, Balfourites, whole hoggers: factionism within the Unionist Party, 1906—1910', *Hist. J.*, XI (no. 1, 1968), 85—124.

797 Brown, John. 'Scottish and English land legislation, 1905—1911', *SHR*, XLVII (Apr. 1968), 72—85.

798 Brown, Kenneth D. 'The Labour Party and the unemployment question, 1906—1910', *Hist. J.*, XIV (no. 3, 1971), 599—616. See also (1519).

799 Chamberlain, Chris. 'The growth of support for the Labour Party in Britain', *BJS*, XXIV (Dec. 1973), 474—89. Sociological study of Labour Party's growth in the 1920s.

800 Clarke, Peter F. 'The end of laissez-faire and the politics of cotton', *Hist. J.*, XV (no. 3, 1972), 493—512.

801 Close, David. 'Conservatives and coalition after the First World War', *JMH*, XLV (June 1973), 240—60.

802 Cole, Margaret. 'Guild socialism and the Labour Research Department', *Ess. Lab. Hist.*, 260—83.

803 David, Edward. 'The Liberal Party divided 1916—1918', *Hist. J.*, XIII (no. 3, 1970), 509—32.

804 Douglas, Roy. 'The background to the "Coupon" election arrangements', *EHR*, LXXXVI (Apr. 1971), 318—36.

805 —— 'The National Democratic Party and the British Workers' League', *Hist. J.*, XV (no. 3, 1972), 533—52. Minority attitudes towards the First World War in Labour Party and socialist groups.

806 —— 'Voluntary enlistment in the First World War and the work of the Parliamentary Recruiting Committee', *JMH*, XLII (Dec. 1970), 564—85.

807 Dowse, Robert E. 'The entry of Liberals into the Labour Party, 1910—1920', *YBESR* (Autumn 1961), 78—87.

808 Dowse, Robert E. and John Peel. 'The politics of birth-control', *PS*, XIII (1965), 179—97.

809 Emy, H.V. 'The impact of financial policy on English party politics before 1914', *Hist. J.*, XV (no. 1, 1972), 103—31.

810 Epstein, Leon D. 'British class consciousness and the Labour Party', *JBS*, V (May, 1962), 136—50.

811 —— 'New M.P.'s and the politics of the PLP', *PS*, X (1962), 121—9. Study of the Parliamentary Labour Party since 1952.

812 —— 'The nuclear deterrent and the British election of 1964', *JBS*, V (no. 2, 1966), 139—63.

813 Fanning, J.R. 'The Unionist Party and Ireland, 1906—1910', *IHS*, XV (Sept. 1966), 147—71.

814 Fraser, Peter. 'The Unionist debacle of 1911 and Balfour's retirement', *JMH*, XXXV (Dec. 1963), 354—65.

815 —— 'Unionism and tariff reform: the crisis of 1906', *Hist. J.*, V (no. 2, 1962), 149—66.

816 Galbraith, John S. 'The pamphlet campaign on the Boer War', *JMH*, XXIV (June 1952), 111—26.

817 Gilbert, Bentley B. 'Health and politics: the physical deterioration report of 1904', *Bulletin of the History of Medicine*, XXXIX (1965), 143—53.

818 —— 'Winston Churchill versus the Webbs: the origins of British unemployment insurance', *AHR*, LXXI (Apr. 1966), 846—62.

819 Golant, W. 'C.R. Attlee in the first and second Labour governments', *Parliamentary Affairs*, XXVI (Summer 1973), 318—35.

820 —— 'The emergence of C.R. Attlee as leader of the Parliamentary Labour Party in 1935', *Hist. J.*, XIII (no. 2, 1970), 318—32.

821 Goldman, Aaron L. 'Defence regulation 18 B: emergency internment of aliens and political dissenters in Great Britain during World War II', *JBS*, XII (May 1973), 120—36.

822 Gooch, John. 'The Maurice debate 1918', *JCH*, III (Oct. 1968), 211—28.

823   Graubard, Stephen Richards. 'Military demobilization in Great Britain follow-
       ing the First World War', *JMH*, XIX (Dec. 1947), 297—311.
824   Harris, José F. and Cameron Hazlehurst. 'Campbell-Bannerman as prime
       minister', *History*, new ser., LV (Oct. 1970), 360—83.
825   Harrison, Royden. 'Labour Government: then and now', *Political Quarterly*,
       XLI (1970), 67—82. Comparison of Labour in 1930 with 1970.
826   —— 'The War Emergency Workers' National Committee, 1914—1920', *Ess.
       Lab. Hist.*, 211—59.
827   Hazlehurst, Cameron. 'Asquith as a prime minister, 1908—1916', *EHR*,
       LXXXV (July 1970), 502—31.
828   Heller, Richard. 'East Fulham revisited', *JCH*, VI (no. 3, 1971), 172—96.
829   Hobsbawm, Eric J. 'The British Communist Party', *Political Quarterly*, XXV
       (no. 1, 1954), 30—43. General information.
830   'Ireland and British politics, 1914—21', *JBS*, XII (Nov. 1971). This sym-
       posium includes: David W. Savage, 'The Parnell of Wales has become the
       Chamberlain of England: Lloyd George and the Irish question', pp. 86—
       108; John M. McEwen, 'The Liberal Party and the Irish question during
       the First World War., pp. 109—131; John D. Fair, 'The Anglo-Irish Treaty
       of 1921 — Unionist aspects of the Peace', pp. 132—49.
831   Jacobson, Peter D. 'Rosebery and Liberal Imperialism 1899—1903', *JBS*, XIII
       (Nov. 1973), 83—107.
832   Kelley, Robert. 'Asquith at Paisley: the content of British Liberalism at the
       end of its era', *JBS*, IV (Nov. 1964), 133—59.
833   Kendle, J.E. 'The Round Table Movement and Home Rule all round', *Hist. J.*,
       XI (no. 2, 1968), 332—53.
834   Kennedy, Thomas C. 'Public opinion and the conscientious objector, 1915—
       1919', *JBS*, XII (May 1973), 105—19.
835   Koss, Stephen E. 'Lloyd George and nonconformity: the last rally', *EHR*,
       LXXXIX (Jan. 1974), 77—108. Concerning 'The Council of Action' move-
       ment, 1935.
836   Layton, Henry. 'The young Conservatives 1945—70', *JCH*, VIII (Apr. 1973),
       143—56.
837   Lockwood, P.A. 'Milner's entry into the War Cabinet, December 1916', *Hist.
       J.*, VII (no. 1, 1964), 120—34.
838   Loewenberg, Gerhard. 'The transformation of the British Labour Party since
       1945', *Journal of Politics*, XXI (May 1959), 234—57.
839   Lyman, Richard W. 'The British Labour Party; the conflict between socialist
       ideals and practical politics between the wars', *JBS*, V (Nov. 1965), 140—
       52.
840   —— 'James Ramsay MacDonald and the leadership of the Labour Party,
       1918—1922', *JBS*, II (Nov. 1962), 132—60.
841   McCready, Herbert W. 'Home Rule and the Liberal Party, 1899—1906', *IHS*,
       XIII (Sept. 1963), 316—48.
842   McDermott, W.J. 'The immediate origins of the Committee of Imperial
       Defence: a reappraisal', *Canadian Journal of History*, VII (Dec. 1972),
       253—72. Based on documentary research.
843   McEwen, J.M. 'The coupon election of 1918 and Unionist members of par-
       liament', *JMH*, XXXIV (Sept. 1962), 294—306.
844   McGill, Barry. 'Asquith's predicament, 1914—1918', *JMH*, XXXIX (Sept.
       1967), 283—303.
845   McKibbin, R.I. 'James Ramsay MacDonald and the problem of the indepen-
       dence of the Labour Party, 1910—1914', *JMH*, XLII (June 1970), 216—
       35. Study of 'MacDonald's leadership in relation both to liberalism and to
       the labor movement'.
846   Mackintosh, J.P. 'The role of the Committee of Imperial Defence before
       1914', *EHR*, LXXVII (July 1962), 490—503.
847   McLean, Iain. 'The rise and fall of the Scottish National Party', *PS*, XVIII
       (1970), 357—72.
848   Marder, Arthur J. 'Winston is back: Churchill at the Admiralty 1939—1940',
       EHR, supplement, V (1972). Cf. Roskill, Stephen W. 'Marder, Churchill
       and the Admiralty 1939—42', *Journal of the Royal United Service*

Institute for Defense Studies, CXVII (Dec. 1972), 49—53; also Roskill's comment in *The Times Literary Supplement*, 13 Dec. 1974, pp. 1415—16.

849 Marwick, Arthur J.B. 'The Independent Labour Party in the nineteen-twenties', *BIHR*, XXXV (1962), 62—74. Uses unpublished material.

850 —— 'James Maxton: his place in Scottish labour history', *SHR*, XLIII (Apr. 1964), 25—43.

851 —— 'Middle opinion in the thirties: planning, progress and political "agreement" ', *EHR*, LXXIX (Apr. 1964), 285—98.

852 —— 'The Labour Party and the welfare state in Britain, 1900—1948', *AHR*, LXXIII (Dec. 1967), 380—403.

853 Mason, A. 'The government and the general strike, 1926', *IRSH*, XIV (pt. 1, 1969), 1—21.

854 Mitchell, David. 'A ghost of a chance: British revolutionaries in 1919', *History Today*, XX (Nov. 1970), 753—61. Carefully researched.

855 Morgan, Kenneth O. 'The New Liberalism and the challenge of Labour: the Welsh experience 1885—1929', *Welsh History Review*, VI (June 1973), 288—312.

856 Morris, Andrew J. Anthony. 'The English Radicals' campaign for disarmament and the Hague Conference of 1907', *JMH*, XLIII (Sept. 1971), 367—93.

857 —— 'Haldane's army reforms 1906—8: the deception of the Radicals', *History*, new ser., LVI (1971), 17—34.

858 Mowat, Charles Loch. 'Baldwin restored', *JMH*, XXVII (June 1955), 169—174. A review article. For subsequent treatment see (744, 828, 875).

859 —— 'The fall of the Labour Government in Great Britain, August, 1931', *Huntington Library Quarterly*, VII (Aug. 1944), 353—86.

860 —— 'Ramsay MacDonald and the Labour Party', *Ess. Lab. Hist.*, 129—51.

861 Murray, Bruce K. 'The politics of the "People's Budget" ', *Hist. J.*, XVI (Sept. 1973), 555—70.

862 Petter, Martin. 'The Progressive Alliance', *History*, LVIII (Feb. 1973), 45—59.

863 Pimlott, Ben. 'The Socialist League: intellectuals and the Labour left in the 1930's', *JCH*, VI (no. 3, 1971), 12—38.

864 Poe, Bryce, II. 'British army reforms, 1902—1914', *Military Affairs*, XXXI (Fall 1967), 131—8. A clear statement.

865 Pollard, Sidney. 'The foundation of the Co-operative Party', *Ess. Lab. Hist.*, 185—210.

866 Prynn, D.L. 'Common Wealth — a British "third party" of the 1940s', *JCH*, VII (nos. 1—2, 1972), 169—79.

867 Rasmussen, Jorgen Scott. 'Government and intra-party opposition: dissent within the Conservative Parliamentary Party in the 1930s', *PS*, XIX (1971), 172—83.

868 Rempel, Richard A. 'Lord Hugh Cecil's parliamentary career, 1900—1914: promise unfulfilled', *JBS*, XI (May 1972), 104—30.

869 Richards, Noel J. 'The Education Bill of 1906 and the decline of political nonconformity', *Journal of Ecclesiastical History*, XXIII (Jan. 1972), 49—63.

870 Round Table. 'Empire to Commonwealth 1910—1970', *Round Table*, Diamond Jubilee Number, no. 240 (Nov. 1970), 375—617. Articles by specialists.

871 Shapiro, Stanley. 'The Great War and reform: Liberals and Labor, 1917—1919', *Labor History*, XII (Summer 1971), 323—44.

872 Sires, Ronald V. 'The beginnings of British legislation for old-age pensions', *JEcH*, XIV (no. 3, 1954), 229—53.

873 Slaughter, C. 'The strike of Yorkshire mineworkers in May, 1955', *Sociological Review*, new ser., VI (Dec. 1958), 241—59. Analysis of an unofficial strike.

874 Smith, John H. and T.E. Chester. 'The distribution of power in nationalised industries', *BJS*, II (Sept. 1951), 275—93.

875 Stannage, C.T. 'The East Fulham by-election, 25 October 1933', *Hist. J.*, XIV (no. 1, 1971), 165—200.

876 Stubbs, J.O. 'Lord Milner and patriotic labour, 1914—1918', *EHR*, LXXXVII (Oct. 1972), 717—54. A study of Milner and the British Workers League.

877   Taylor, H.A. 'The proportional decline hypothesis in English elections',
      Journal of the Royal Statistical Society, ser. A, CXXXV (1972), 365—9.
      Tested from General Elections 1950—70.
878   Tsuzuki, Chushichi. 'The "Impossibilist Revolt" in Britain', *IRSH*, I (pt. 3,
      1956), 377—97. Origins of the Socialist Labour Party and of the Socialist
      Party of Great Britain, 1900—4.
879   Tucker, Albert. 'The issue of army reform in the Unionist Government,
      1903—5', *Hist. J.*, IX (no. 1, 1966), 90—100.
880   Walker, William M. 'Dundee's disenchantment with Churchill: a comment
      upon the downfall of the Liberal Party', *SHR*, XLIX (Apr. 1970), 85—
      108.
881   Watt, David. 'The politics of 1951—71', *History Today*, XXII (Jan. 1972),
      3—11. Study of the impact of 'mass democracy'.
882   Winter, J.M. 'Arthur Henderson, the Russian Revolution and the reconstruc-
      tion of the Labour Party', *Hist. J.*, XV (no. 4, 1972), 753—73.

VI. FOREIGN RELATIONS

1 Printed sources

884   Angell, Norman. *The great illusion: a study of the relation of military power
      in nations to their economic and social advantage*. 1910. Revision of his
      Europe's optical illusion. 1909. A classic.
885   Barman, Thomas. *Diplomatic correspondent*. 1968. As correspondent for the
      BBC, 1946—67.
886   Buchanan, George. *My mission to Russia and other diplomatic memories*.
      1923. 2 vols. Buchanan was ambassador to Tsarist Russia and to Italy.
887   Craigie, Robert. *Behind the Japanese mask*. [1946]. A significant account by
      the ambassador to Japan 1937—42.
888   d'Abernon, Edgar Vincent, Viscount. *Diary of an ambassador*. 1929—31, 3
      vols.
889   Dickinson, G. Lowes. *The international anarchy, 1904—1914*. 1936. By a
      humanist, historian and philosophical writer.
890   Dilks, David (ed.). *The diaries of Sir Alexander Cadogan O.M., 1938—1945*.
      1971. Cadogan was permanent under-secretary in the Foreign Office.
891   Eayrs, James (ed.). *The Commonwealth and Suez: a documentary survey*.
      1964.
892   Evans, Trefor E. (ed.). *The Killearn Diaries, 1934—1946*. 1972. Lord Killearn
      (Sir Miles Lampson) was British ambassador to Egypt during World War II.
893   Gilbert, Martin. *Britain and Germany between the wars*. 1964. Short extracts
      from various documents.
894   Gladwyn, Hubert Miles Gladwyn Jebb, Baron. *Memoirs of Lord Gladwyn*.
      1972.
895   Glubb, John Bagot. *Britain and the Arabs: a study of fifty years, 1908—1958*.
      1959. By the officer commanding the Arab Legion in Jordan.
896   Gooch, George P. and Temperley, Harold W.V. (eds.). *British documents on
      the origins of the war, 1898—1914*. 1926—38, 11 vols. Standard.
897   Grenville, J.A.S. (ed.). *The major international treaties 1914—1973. A history
      and guide with texts*. 1974. Invaluable.
898   Grey, Edward, Viscount Grey of Falloden. *Speeches on foreign affairs, 1904—
      1914*, ed. Paul Knaplund. 1931.
899   —— *Twenty-five years, 1892—1916*. New York, 1925, 2 vols. By the foreign
      secretary, 1905—16.
900   Gwynn, Stephen (ed.). *The letters and friendships of Sir Cecil Spring Rice*.
      1930, 2 vols. Spring Rice was ambassador to the U.S.A., 1913—18.
901   Hachey, Thomas E. (ed.). *Anglo-Vatican relations, 1914—1919: confidential*

annual reports of the British ministers to the Holy See. Boston, Mass., 1972.

902   Hankey, Maurice P.A., 1st Baron. *The supreme control at the Paris Peace Conference, 1919: a commentary.* 1963.

903   Hardinge, Charles, Baron. *Old diplomacy: the reminiscences of Lord Hardinge of Penshurst.* 1947.

904   Harvey, John (ed.). *Diplomatic diaries of Oliver Harvey 1937–1940.* 1970. Harvey was private secretary to Eden and Halifax.

905   Headlam-Morley, James. *A memoir of the Paris Peace Conference 1919*, ed. Agnes Headlam-Morley *et al.* 1972.

906   Henderson, Nevile. *Failure of a mission: Berlin 1937–1939.* New York, 1940. See also (1103).

907   Hoare, Samuel J.G., Viscount Templewood. *Ambassador on special mission.* 1946. Mission to Spain 1940–4.

908   Howard, Esme, Lord Howard of Penrith. *Theatre of life.* Boston, Mass., 1935–6, 2 vols. Howard was in the Foreign Service 1885–1930; was ambassador to the U.S.A., 1924–30.

909   Kirkpatrick, Ivone. *The inner circle.* 1959. Memoirs; Kirkpatrick was high commissioner to Germany 1950–3 and permanent undersecretary of foreign affairs, 1953–7.

910   Knatchbull-Hugessen, Hughe. *Diplomat in peace and war.* 1949. Ambassador to China, Turkey and Belgium.

911   Koss, Stephen E. (ed.). *The anatomy of an antiwar movement: the pro-Boers.* Chicago, 1973. Readings with commentary.

912   Lawrence, Thomas E. *Seven pillars of wisdom: a triumph.* 1925. An abbreviated version in *Revolt in the desert.* 1927.

913   Lennox, Lady Algernon Gordon (ed.). *The diary of Lord Bertie of Thame, 1914–1918.* N.d., 2 vols. Bertie was ambassador to Italy, 1903–4 and to France 1905–18.

914   Leslie, Shane. *Mark Sykes: his life and letters.* 1923. Sykes was chiefly responsible for the 'Sykes-Picot' agreement of 1916.

915   Lloyd George, David. *The truth about the peace treaties.* 1938, 2 vols. In the U.S.A. published as *Memoirs of the peace conference.* New Haven, Conn., 1939, 2 vols.

916   Lockhart, Bruce. *British agent.* New York, 1933. On his activities in Malaya, Poland, Czecho-Slovakia. Published in England as *Memoirs of a British agent.* 1932.

917   Lugard, Frederick John Dealtry, Baron. *Political memoranda: revision of instructions to political officers on subjects chiefly political and administrative 1913–1918.* 1970. Lugard was governor-general of Nigeria 1914–1919. See also (1101).

918   Morel, E.D. *Truth and the war.* 1916. Reprint with introduction by Catherine Ann Cline, New York, 1972.

919   Nicolson, Harold. *Peacemaking 1919: being reminiscences of the Paris Peace Conference.* Boston, Mass., 1933. Nicolson served with the British delegation.

920   Ponsonby, Arthur, Baron. *Democracy and diplomacy – a plea for popular control of foreign policy.* 1915. Ponsonby, a life-long pacifist, was a Radical Liberal (later, a Laborite) in politics.

921   Riddell, George Allardice, Baron. *Intimate diary of the Peace Conference and after.* 1933. Riddell was a newspaper proprietor and confidant of Lloyd George.

922   *Stalin's correspondence with Churchill, Attlee, Roosevelt and Truman, 1941–45.* 1958.

923   Strang, William, 1st Baron. *Home and abroad.* 1956. An account of a significant role in the Foreign Office, 1919–53. See also (1066).

924   Strong, Kenneth. *Intelligence at the top; the recollections of an intelligence officer.* 1968. He was head of General Eisenhower's Intelligence staff, 1943–5.

925   Temperley, Arthur C. *The whispering gallery of Europe.* 1938. By the military adviser at Geneva to the British foreign secretary, 1923–38.

926 Vansittart, Robert Gilbert, 1st Baron. *The mist procession*. 1958. Autobiography (to 1936) of a noted diplomat; he was permanent undersecretary in the Foreign Office, 1930—8.
927 Watt, Donald Cameron and James Mayall (eds.). *Current British foreign policy 1970—*. 1972—. An annual reference work of documents; thus far volumes have appeared for 1970, 1971 and 1972.
928 Watt, Donald C. *Documents on the Suez crisis*. 1957. Selected documents with commentary.
929 Wheeler-Bennett, John W. *et al.* (eds.). *Documents on international affairs*. 1929—73. An annual series for the years 1928—1963, by various editors, sponsored by the Royal Institute of International Affairs.
930 Woodward, Ernest Llewellyn and William N. Medlicott *et al.* (eds.). *Documents on British foreign policy 1919—1939*. Three series. 1947—. A basic collection, in progress; documents from the Foreign Office archives. The latest volume was published in 1973. See also (1124).

2 Surveys

931 Barker, Elisabeth. *Britain in a divided Europe, 1945—1970*. 1971.
932 Collins, Doreen. *Aspects of British politics 1904—1919*. 1965.
933 Foot, Michael R.D. *British foreign policy since 1898*. 1956.
934 Gooch, George P. 'British foreign policy, 1919—1939', in his *Studies in diplomacy and statecraft*. 1942, pp. 86—107. Brilliant.
935 Haigh, Anthony. *Congress of Vienna to Common Market: an outline of British foreign policy 1815—1972*. 1973. Largely on the twentieth century.
936 Medlicott, William N. *British foreign policy since Versailles 1919—1963*. 2nd ed., 1968. A standard work.
937 Northedge, Frederick S. *British foreign policy: the process of readjustment 1945—1961*. 1962.
938 —— *The troubled giant: Britain among the powers 1916—1939*. 1966.
939 Platt, Desmond C.M. *Finance, trade and politics in British foreign policy, 1815—1914*. Oxford, 1968.
940 Reynolds, Philip A. *British foreign policy in the inter-war years*. 1954.
941 Toynbee, Arnold J. *et al. Survey of international affairs*. 1925—. Begins with 1920; the most recent volume is for 1962 (1970). Consolidated index volume, 1920—38 (1967).
942 Ward, Adolphus W. and George P. Gooch (eds.). *Cambridge history of British foreign policy 1783—1919*. Vol. III, *1866—1919*. Cambridge, 1923.
943 Woodhouse, Christopher M. *British foreign policy since the Second World War*. 1961.

3 Monographs

944 Allen, Harry C. *The Anglo-American predicament: the British Commonwealth, the United States and European unity*. 1960. Revision and enlargement of Part I of his *Great Britain and the United States 1783—1952*. 1954.
945 Arnot, R. Page. *The impact of the Russian Revolution in Britain*. 1967.
946 Bartlett, Christopher J. *The long retreat: a short history of British defence policy 1945—70*. 1972.
947 Bassett, Reginald. *Democracy and foreign policy: a case history, the Sino-Japanese dispute 1931—33*. 1952. Cf. (1075).
948 Beloff, Max. *Lucien Wolf and the Anglo-Russian Entente 1907—1914*. 1951. A lecture.
949 —— *New dimensions in foreign policy: a study in administrative experience, 1947—1959*. 1961. Study of the impact of international organization on the administration and political systems of independent states.
950 Bennett, Jeremy. *British broadcasting and the Danish Resistance movement, 1940—1945*. 1966.
951 Boardman, Robert and A.J.R. Groom (eds.). *The management of Britain's*

external relations. 1973. Chapters by various writers. Investigates questions growing out of Britain's changing international position since 1945.

952 Braddon, Russell. *Suez: splitting of a nation*. 1973. What Suez meant to the British people.

953 Brebner, John Bartlet. *North Atlantic triangle: the interplay of Canada, the United States and Great Britain*. New Haven, Conn., 1945.

954 Bridge, F.R. *Great Britain and Austria-Hungary, 1906–1914*: a diplomatic history. 1972. See also (1110).

955 Busch, Briton Cooper. *Britain, India, and the Arabs, 1914–1921*. Berkeley, Cal., 1971.

956 ——— *Britain and the Persian Gulf, 1894–1914*. Berkeley, Cal., 1967.

957 Carlton, David. *MacDonald versus Henderson: the foreign policy of the second Labour Government*. New York, 1970. See also (1031).

958 Carr, Edward H. *Britain: a study of foreign policy from the Versailles Treaty to the outbreak of war*. 1939. Brief essay; interesting observations representing a pre-war view of a noted historian.

959 Carter, Gwendolen M. *The British Commonwealth and international security: the role of the Dominions 1919–1939*. Toronto, 1947.

960 Chapman, Maybelle Kennedy. *Great Britain and the Bagdad Railway, 1888–1914* (Smith College Studies in History, 31). Northampton, Mass., 1948.

961 Chaput, Rolland A. *Disarmament in British foreign policy*. 1935.

962 Churchill, Rogers Platt. *The Anglo-Russian convention of 1907*. Cedar Rapids, Iowa, 1939.

963 Clifford, Nicholas R. *Retreat from China: British policy in the Far East, 1937–1941*. Seattle, Wash., 1967.

964 Coates, William P. and Zelda K. Coates. *Armed intervention in Russia 1918–1922*. 1935. Includes full account of Britain's role.

965 ——— *A history of Anglo-Soviet relations*. 1945, 1958, 2 vols.

966 Collier, Basil. *The lion and the eagle: British and Anglo-American strategy, 1900–1950*. 1972.

967 Collins, Robert O. *King Leopold, England, and the Upper Nile, 1899–1909*. 1968.

968 Colvin, Ian G. *Vansittart in office: an historical survey of the origins of the Second World War based on the papers of Sir Robert Vansittart*. 1965. Published in U.S.A. as *None so blind: a British diplomatic view of the origins of World War II*. New York, 1965.

969 Conwell-Evans, Thomas P. *Foreign policy from a back bench, 1904–1918: a study based on the papers of Lord Noel-Buxton*. 1932. See also Anderson, Mosa, *Noel Buxton: a life*. 1952.

970 Cookey, S.J.S. *Great Britain and the Congo question, 1885–1913*. 1968.

971 Darby, Philip. *British defence policy east of Suez, 1947–1968*. 1973.

972 Dennis, Peter. *Decision by default: peace time conscription and British defence 1919–39*. 1972.

973 D'Ombrain, Nicholas. *War machinery and high policy: defence administration in peacetime Britain 1902–1914*. 1973.

974 Epstein, Leon D. *Britain — uneasy ally*. Chicago, Ill., 1954. Anglo-American relations, 1945–1952.

975 ——— *British politics in the Suez crisis*. 1964.

976 Fabunmi, L.A. *The Sudan in Anglo-Egyptian relations: a case study in power politics, 1880–1956*. 1960. Largely on the twentieth century.

977 Fitzsimons, Matthew A. *Empire by treaty: Britain and the Middle East in the twentieth century*. 1965.

978 ——— *The foreign policy of the British Labour government, 1945–1951*. Notre Dame, Indiana, 1953.

979 Fowler, W.B. *British–American relations 1917–18: the role of Sir William Wiseman*. Princeton, N.J., 1969. Wiseman was the Foreign Office liaison officer in the U.S.A.

980 Friedman, Irving S. *British relations with China: 1931–1939*. New York, 1940.

981 Friedman, Isaiah. *The question of Palestine, 1914–1918: British-Jewish-Arab relations*. 1973.

982 Gannon, Franklin Reid. *The British press and Germany 1936—1939*. Oxford, 1971.
983 Gelber, Lionel M. *The rise of Anglo-American friendship: a study in world politics 1898—1906*. 1938.
984 George, Margaret. *The warped vision: British foreign policy 1933—1939*. Pittsburgh, Pa., 1965. Based on printed sources.
985 Gifford, Prosser and William Roger Louis (eds.). *Britain and Germany in Africa: imperial rivalry and colonial rule*. New Haven, Conn., 1967. Papers originally presented at a Conference at Yale University in 1965. See also their *France and Britain in Africa: imperial rivalry and colonial rule*. New Haven, 1971. Papers originally presented at Yale University in 1968.
986 Gilbert, Martin. *The roots of appeasement*. 1966. Study of period, 1914—39.
987 Gooch, George P. *Before the war: studies in diplomacy*. 1936—8, 2 vols. Vol. II, pp. 3—133 has an important assessment of Sir Edward Grey.
988 Goodhart, Philip. *Fifty ships that saved the world: the foundations of the Anglo-American alliance*. 1965. Concerning the agreement of 1940 on bases and destroyers.
989 Goodwin, Geoffrey L. *Britain and the United Nations*. New York, 1957. On the period 1943—56, from printed sources.
990 Gordon, Michael R. *Conflict and consensus in Labour's foreign policy 1914—1965*. Stanford, Cal., 1969. Emphasis on post 1945. A controversial subject.
991 Gottlieb, Wolfram W. *Studies in secret diplomacy during the First World War*. 1957.
992 *Great Britain and Egypt, 1914—1951*. Information Papers, no. 19, Royal Institute of International Affairs. 1936. New and rev. ed., 1952.
993 *Great Britain and Palestine, 1915—1945*. Information Papers, no. 20, Royal Institute of International Affairs. 1946.
994 Hale, Oron James. *Publicity and diplomacy, with special reference to England and Germany, 1890—1914*. 1940. A significant study.
995 Halpern, Paul G. *The Mediterranean naval situation 1908—1914*. Cambridge, Mass., 1971. Archival study of the policy of Britain and others.
996 Hanak, Harry. *Great Britain and Austria-Hungary during the first World War: a study in the formation of public opinion*. 1962.
997 Hauser, Oswald. *England und das Dritte Reich*. Erster band, *1933 bis 1936*. Stuttgart, 1972. Based on British archival material.
998 Higham, Robin D.S. *The military intellectuals in Britain: 1918—1939*. New Brunswick, N.J., 1966.
999 Hollingsworth, Lawrence W. *Zanzibar under the Foreign Office, 1890—1913*. 1953.
1000 Jordan, William M. *Great Britain, France and the German problem, 1918—1939*. 1943. Thorough and scholarly.
1001 Kazemazadeh, Firuz. *Russia and Britain in Persia, 1864—1914: a study in imperialism*. New Haven, Conn., 1968.
1002 Kedourie, Elie. *England and the Middle East: the destruction of the Ottoman Empire, 1914—1921*. 1956.
1003 Kennedy, John F. *Why England slept*. 1940. A study of the 1930s which attracted wide attention.
1004 Kennedy, Malcolm D. *The estrangement of Great Britain and Japan, 1917—35*. Manchester, 1969.
1005 Klieman, Aaron S. *Foundations of British policy in the Arab world: the Cairo Conference of 1921*. Baltimore, Md., 1970.
1006 Lammers, Donald Ned. *British foreign policy, 1929—1934: the problem of Soviet Russia*. Stanford, Cal., 1960.
1007 —— *Explaining Munich: the search for motive in British policy* (Hoover Institution Studies, 16). Stanford, Cal., 1966.
1008 Lee, Bradford A. *Britain and the Sino-Japanese war 1937—1939: a study in the dilemmas of British decline*. Stanford, Cal., 1973. A fine piece of scholarship, including an invaluable bibliographical note.
1009 Le May, Godfrey H.L. *British supremacy in South Africa, 1899—1907*. Oxford, 1965.

1010   Louis, William Roger. *British strategy in the Far East, 1919–1939*. Oxford, 1971.
1011   —— *Great Britain and Germany's lost colonies, 1914–1919*. Oxford, 1967.
1012   Lowe, Cedric J. and Dockrill, M.L. *The mirage of power: British foreign policy 1902–22*. 1972, 3 vols. Documents in vol. III.
1013   Lowe, Peter. *Great Britain and Japan 1911–1915: a study of British Far Eastern policy*. 1969.
1014   Luard, Evan. *Britain and China*. Baltimore, Md., 1962. Useful survey since 1945.
1015   Lyddon, William G. *British war missions to the United States 1914–1918*. 1938.
1016   McDermott, Geoffrey. *The Eden legacy and the decline of British diplomacy*. 1969. Suez (1956) and after — an indictment.
1017   Maclean, Donald. *British foreign policy: the years since Suez, 1956–1968*. 1970.
1018   McNeill, William Hardy. *America, Britain and Russia, their co-operation and conflict 1941–1946*. 1953. Outstanding volume in *Survey of International Affairs, 1939–1946*, ed. Arnold Toynbee.
1019   Maddox, William P. *Foreign relations in British Labour politics . . . 1900–1924*. Cambridge, Mass., 1934.
1020   Mander, John. *Great Britain or little England?* 1963. Examined in a historical context.
1021   Manderson-Jones, Ronald B. *The special relationship: Anglo-American relations and western unity 1947–56*. New York, 1972.
1022   Mansfield, Peter. *The British in Egypt*. New York, 1972. A popular account of developments 1882–1956.
1023   Marlowe, John. *A history of modern Egypt and Anglo-Egyptian relations, 1800–1956*. 2nd ed., Hamden, Conn., 1965.
1024   Martin, David A. *Pacifism: an historical and sociological study*. New York, 1965. With particular reference to Britain 1914–45; excellent bibliography.
1025   Martin, Laurence W. *Peace without victory; Woodrow Wilson and the British Liberals*. New Haven, Conn., 1958.
1026   Masterman, John C. *The double-cross system in the war of 1939 to 1945*. 1972. An account of British intelligence.
1027   Mathews, Joseph James. *Egypt and the formation of the Anglo-French Entente of 1904*. Philadelphia, Pa., 1939.
1028   Medlicott, William N. *Britain and Germany: the search for agreement 1930–1937*. 1969. Creighton lecture, 1968.
1029   Meehan, Eugene J. *The British left wing and foreign policy: a study of the influence of ideology*. New Brunswick, N.J., 1960. During World War II and on to 1951.
1030   Middlemas, Keith. *Diplomacy of illusion: the British government and Germany, 1937–39*. 1972.
1031   Miller, Kenneth E. *Socialism and foreign policy: theory and practice in Britain to 1931*. The Hague, 1967. For discussion of the issues, see Barbara Malament in *JMH*, XLII (June 1970), 280–4.
1032   Monger, George. *The end of isolation; British foreign policy, 1900–1907*. 1963.
1033   Monroe, Elizabeth. *Britain's moment in the Middle East 1914–1956*. 1963.
1034   Montgelas, Maximilian Garnerin, Count. *British foreign policy under Sir Edward Grey*, tr. William C. Dreher, ed. Harry Elmer Barnes. New York, 1928. An influential book during the years of revisionism.
1035   Naylor, John F. *Labour's international policy: The Labour Party in the 1930s*. Boston, 1969. Detail rather than analysis.
1036   Nelson, Harold I. *Land and power: British and allied policy on Germany's frontiers, 1916–19*. 1963. Concerning the territorial settlement at the Paris Peace Conference.
1037   Nevakivi, Jukka. *Britain, France and the Arab Middle East, 1914–1920*. 1969.

1038   Nicholas, Herbert George. *Britain and the U.S.A.* Baltimore, Md., 1963. On period 1938–1960.
1039   Nicolson, Harold. *Curzon: the last phase, 1919–1925: a study in post-war diplomacy.* 1934.
1040   Nimocks, Walter. *Milner's young men: the 'kindergarten' in Edwardian imperial affairs.* Durham, N.C., 1968.
1041   Nish, Ian H. *Alliance in decline: a study in Anglo-Japanese relations, 1908–23.* 1972. This story continued in (1010).
1042   —— *The Anglo-Japanese alliance; the diplomacy of two island empires, 1894–1907.* 1966. Nish's work is learned and skilful.
1043   Nutting, Anthony. *No end of a lesson: the story of Suez.* 1967. One of the best accounts.
1044   Padfield, Peter. *The great naval race: the Anglo-German naval rivalry 1900–1914.* 1974. See also (1091).
1045   Parkinson, Roger. *Peace for our time: Munich to Dunkirk, the inside story.* 1971.
1046   Perkins, Bradford. *The great rapprochement; England and the United States, 1895–1914.* 1969. An admirable synthesis.
1047   Plass, Jens B. *England zwischen Russland und Deutschland: der persische Golf in der britischen Vorkriegspolitik, 1889–1907.* Hamburg, 1966.
1048   Porter, Brian. *Britain and the rise of Communist China: a study of British attitudes 1945–1954.* 1967.
1049   Pribram, Alfred Francis. *Austria-Hungary and Great Britain, 1908–1914*, tr. Ian F.D. Morrow. 1921. See also Pribram's *England and the international policy of the European Great Powers 1871–1914.* (Ford Lectures, 1929). 1931.
1050   Price, Richard. *An imperial war and the British working class: working class attitudes and reactions to the Boer War, 1899–1902.* 1972. Inconclusive.
1051   Rappaport, Armin. *The British press and Wilsonian neutrality.* Stanford, Cal., 1951.
1052   Reid, Robert Threshie, Earl Loreburn. *How the war came.* 1919. As it appeared to the lord chancellor in the Liberal Government 1905–12.
1053   Richardson, J. Henry. *British economic foreign policy.* 1936. Useful for 1918–.
1054   Robbins, Keith. *Munich, 1938.* 1968. Includes thorough analysis of British policy.
1055   Robertson, Terence. *Crisis: the inside story of the Suez conspiracy.* 1965. Somewhat journalistic but well informed.
1056   Rock, William R. *Appeasement on trial: British foreign policy and its critics, 1938–1939.* Hamden, Conn., 1966.
1057   Rolo, P.J.V. *Entente Cordiale: the origins and negotiation of the Anglo-French agreements of 8 April, 1904.* 1969.
1058   Rose, N.A. *The gentile Zionists: a study in Anglo-Zionist diplomacy, 1929–1939.* 1973.
1059   Rose, Saul. *Britain and South-east Asia.* Baltimore, Md., 1962. Emphasis on twentieth-century developments.
1060   Rothstein, Andrew. *British foreign policy and its critics, 1830–1950.* 1969. Communist interpretation of the ideas of W.S. Blunt, Robert Dell and E.D. Morel.
1061   Rothwell, Victor H. *British war aims and peace diplomacy, 1914–1918.* Oxford, 1971.
1062   Rowse, A. Leslie. *All Souls and appeasement.* 1961. 'Evidence', not 'history', Rowse calls it. Published in the U.S.A. as *Appeasement: a study in political decline 1933–1939.* New York, 1963.
1063   Shwadran, Benjamin. *The Middle East, oil and the great powers.* 2nd ed., 1959.
1064   Stein, Leonard. *The Balfour Declaration.* 1961. Concerning the promise that Palestine would be a national home for Jews.
1065   Steiner, Zara S. *The Foreign Office and foreign policy, 1898–1914.* 1969.
1066   Strang, William, 1st Baron. *The diplomatic career.* 1962. Public addresses.
1067   Strong, Kenneth. *Men of Intelligence: a study of the roles and decisions of*

chiefs of intelligence from World War I to the present day. 1970. See also (924).

1068   Sykes, Christopher. *Crossroads to Israel.* New York, 1965. On Great Britain and Zionism.

1069   Taylor, Alan J.P. *The Origins of the Second World War.* 1961. 2nd ed., 'with a reply to critics', n.d. See comment by T.W. Mason, 'Some origins of the Second World War', *PP*, XXIX (Dec. 1964), 67–87 and Taylor's reply, 'War origins again', *PP*, XXX (Apr. 1965), 110–13.

1070   Temperley, Harold W.V. (ed.). *History of the Peace Conference of Paris.* 1920–4, 6 vols. A comprehensive and impressive history.

1071   Thomas, Hugh. *The Spanish Civil War.* 1961. Includes full account of British policy.

1072   —— *The Suez affair.* 1967. In the U.S.A. as *Suez.* New York, 1967. The crisis of 1956.

1073   Thompson, Neville. *The anti-appeasers.* 1971. Points out inconsistencies in Conservative opposition to appeasement in the 1930s.

1074   Thorne, Christopher G. *The approach of war, 1938–1939.* 1967.

1075   —— *The limits of foreign policy: the West, the League and the Far Eastern crisis, 1931–1933.* 1972. Follows Britain's role carefully. Supersedes (947).

1076   Tillman, Seth P. *Anglo-American relations at the Paris Peace Conference of 1919.* Princeton, N.J., 1961.

1077   Tucker, William Rayburn. *The attitude of the British Labour Party towards European and collective security problems 1920–1939.* Genève, 1950.

1078   Ullman, Richard H. *Anglo-Soviet relations, 1917–1921.* 1961–72, 3 vols. In the main a study of British politics; as such it is thorough and absorbing.

1079   Waites, Neville (ed.). *Troubled neighbours: Franco-British relations in the twentieth century.* 1971. Articles of general interest by British and French historians.

1080   Walder, David. *The Chanak affair.* 1969. The best treatment of the Anglo-Turkish crisis of 1922.

1081   Watt, Donald Cameron. *Britain looks to Germany; British opinion and policy towards Germany since 1945.* 1965.

1082   —— *Personalities and policies. Studies in the formulation of British foreign policy in the twentieth century.* 1965. Notre Dame, Ind., 1965. Aims 'to bridge gap' between history and political science.

1083   Willert, Arthur. *The road to safety: a study in Anglo-American relations.* 1952. Concerns Sir William Wiseman and British diplomacy in Washington, D.C. during World War I.

1084   Williams Ann. *Britain and France in the Middle East and North Africa, 1914–1967.* 1968. Good general account with excellent bibliography.

1085   Williamson, Samuel R. Jr. *The politics of grand strategy: Britain and France prepare for war, 1904–1914.* Cambridge, Mass., 1969. Probably the best as well as the most complete treatment. Useful description of manuscript collections.

1086   Wilson, Theodore A. *The first summit: Roosevelt and Churchill at Placentia Bay 1941.* Boston, 1969.

1087   Windrich, Elaine. *British Labour's foreign policy.* Stanford, Cal., 1952. Cf. Malament, *JMH*, XLII (June 1970), 280–4.

1088   Winkler, Henry R. *The League of Nations movement in Great Britain.* New Brunswick, N.J., 1952. An important book.

1089   Wolfers, Arnold. *Britain and France between two wars: conflicting strategies of peace since Versailles.* New York, 1940. Reflects the atmosphere of the 1930s.

1090   Woodward, Ernest Llewellyn. *British foreign policy in the second world war.* 1970–1, 3 vols. Part of the 'official history' of the war; clear, comprehensive with complete documentation.

1091   —— *Great Britain and the German navy.* Oxford, 1935. This initial careful study is still very useful. See also (1044).

1092   Zilliacus, Konni. *Mirror of the past: a history of secret diplomacy.* New York, 1946.

FOREIGN RELATIONS

1093   Zimmermann, Walter. *Die englische Presse zum Ausbruch des Weltkrieges.* Berlin, 1928.

4 Biographies
(See also sec. V, pt. 4, above.)

1094   Aldington, Richard. *Lawrence of Arabia: a biographical enquiry.* 1955. A critical examination.
1095   Gilbert, Martin. *Sir Horace Rumbold: portrait of a diplomat 1869–1941.* Rumbold was in turn minister or ambassador to Switzerland, Poland, Turkey, Spain and Germany.
1096   Hendrick, Burton J. *The Life and letters of Walter H. Page.* New York, 1922– 5, 3 vols. Page was the American ambassador to Great Britain 1913–18.
1097   Knightley, Philip and Colin Simpson. *The secret lives of Lawrence of Arabia.* 1969. Attacks the popular conception of Lawrence as pro-Arab.
1098   Liddell Hart, Basil Henry. *'T.E. Lawrence': in Arabia and after.* 1934. Eulogistic. Cf. (1094).
1099   Mosley, Leonard. *Curzon: the end of an epoch.* 1960. Brief, readable; as yet there is no adequate biography of Curzon.
1100   Nicolson, Harold. *Sir Arthur Nicolson, Bart., First Lord Carnock: a study in the old diplomacy.* 1930. Nicolson was ambassador to Russia 1906–10 and under-secretary for foreign affairs, 1910–16.
1101   Perham, Margery F. *Lugard: the years of authority, 1898–1945: the second part of the life of Frederick Dealtry Lugard.* 1960. Lugard was an outstanding colonial administrator. See also (917).
1102   Robbins, Keith. *Sir Edward Grey: a biography of Lord Grey of Falloden.* 1971. On Grey's official role, replaces (776).
1103   Strauch, Rudi. *Sir Nevile Henderson, britischer Botschafter in Berlin von 1937 bis 1939.* Bonn, 1959.
1104   Waterfield, Gordon. *Professional diplomat: Sir Percy Loraine of Kirkharle, Bt., 1880–1961.* 1973. A career diplomat.

5 Articles

1105   Allen, R.G.D. 'Mutual aid between the U.S. and the British Empire, 1941– 45', *Journal of the Royal Statistical Society*, CIX (pt. 3, 1946), 243–77.
1106   Anderson, Edgar. 'British policy toward the Baltic states, 1918–1920', *Journal of Central European Affairs*, XIX (Oct. 1959), 276–89.
1107   Beloff, Max. 'The special relationship: an Anglo-American myth', in Martin Gilbert (ed.). *A Century of Conflict, 1850–1950.* 1966, pp. 151–71.
1108   Bosworth, Richard. 'Britain and Italy's acquisition of the Dodecanese, 1912– 1915', *Hist. J.*, XIII (no. 4, 1970), 683–705.
1109   —— 'The British press, the Conservatives and Mussolini, 1920–34', *JCH*, V (no. 2, 1970), 163–82.
1110   Bridge, F.R. 'The British declaration of war on Austria-Hungary in 1914', *Slavonic and East European Review*, XLVII (July 1969), 401-22. See also (954).
1111   Bury, John P.T. 'Diplomatic history 1900–1912', in *NCMH*, 112–39.
1112   Butterfield, Herbert. 'Sir Edward Grey in July 1914', *Historical Studies* (Papers read before the sixth Conference of Irish Historians), V, (1965), 1–25.
1113   Cairns, John C. 'Great Britain and the fall of France: a study in allied disunity', *JMH*, XXVII (Dec. 1955), 365–409.
1114   Carlton, David. 'The Anglo-French compromise on arms limitation, 1928', *JBS*, VIII (May 1969), 141–62.
1115   —— 'Great Britain and the League Council crisis of 1926', *Hist. J.*, XI (no. 2, 1968), 354–64.
1116   Chandran, J. 'Britain and Siamese Malay States, 1892–1904: a comment', *Hist. J.*, XV (no. 3, 1972), 471–92.
1117   Cline, Catherine Ann. 'E.D. Morel and the crusade against the Foreign Office', *JMH*, XXXIX (June 1967), 126–37.

1118   Coghlan, F. 'Armaments, economic policy and appeasement: background to
        British foreign policy 1931–7', *History*, LVII (no. 2, 1972), 205–16.

1119   Cohen, Michael J. 'Appeasement in the Middle East: the British White Paper
        on Palestine, May 1939', *Hist. J.*, XVI (Sept. 1973), 571–96.

1120   —— 'British strategy and the Palestine question 1936–39', *JCH*, VII (nos.
        3–4, 1972), 157–83. Based on Colonial Office and Cabinet Office papers.

1121   Conway, John S. 'The Vatican, Great Britain and relations with Germany
        1938–1940', *Hist. J.*, XVI (Mar. 1973), 147–67.

1122   Cooper, M.B. 'British policy in the Balkans, 1908–9', *Hist. J.*, VII (no. 2,
        1964), 258–79.

1123   Craig, Gordon A. 'The British Foreign Office from Grey to Austen
        Chamberlain', in Gordon A. Craig and Felix Gilbert (eds.), *The diplomats,
        1919–1939*. Princeton, N.J., 1953, pp. 15–48.

1124   —— 'High tide of appeasement: the road to Munich, 1937–1938', *Political
        Science Quarterly*, LXV (Mar. 1950), 20–37. Critique of (930).

1125   Crowe, Sibyl Eyre. 'Sir Eyre Crowe and the Locarno Pact', *EHR*, LXXXVII
        (Jan. 1972), 49–74.

1126   Dowse, Robert E. 'The Independent Labour Party and foreign politics,
        1918–23', *IRSH*, VII (1962), 33–46.

1127   Dubin, Martin David. 'Toward the concept of collective security: the Bryce
        Group's "Proposals for the Avoidance of War", 1914–1917', *Inter-
        national Organization*, XXIV (1970), 288–318.

1128   Edwards, E.W. 'Great Britain and the Manchurian Railways Question, 1909–
        1910', *EHR*, LXXXI (Oct. 1966), 740–69.

1129   Edwards, Peter. 'The Austen Chamberlain–Mussolini meetings', *Hist. J.*, XIV
        (no. 1, 1971), 153–64. Account of five meetings, 1924–29, based on the
        Chamberlain papers, Cabinet papers, British and Italian Foreign Office
        documents.

1130   Egerton, George W. 'The Lloyd George Government and the creation of the
        League of Nations', *AHR*, LXXIX (Apr. 1974), 419–44. Detailed exam-
        ination on basis of Cabinet and Lloyd George papers.

1131   Elcock, H.J. 'Britain and the Russo-Polish frontier, 1919–1921', *Hist J.*, XII
        (no. 1, 1969), 137–54.

1132   Fest, W.B. 'British war aims and German peace feelers during the First World
        War (December 1916 – November 1918)', *Hist. J.*, XV (no. 2, 1972),
        285–308.

1133   Fieldhouse, H.N. 'Noel Buxton and A.J.P. Taylor's "The Troublemakers" ',
        in Martin Gilbert (ed.). *A century of conflict, 1850–1950*. 1966, pp.
        175–98.

1134   Fox, John P. 'Britain and the Inter-allied Military Commission of Control',
        JCH, IV (Apr. 1969), 143–64. Based on Foreign Office and Cabinet
        documents.

1135   Fry, M.G. 'The North Atlantic triangle and the abrogation of the Anglo-
        Japanese Alliance', *JMH*, XXXIX (Mar. 1967), 46–64. Concerning events
        in 1920–1.

1136   Gibbs, Norman. 'British strategic doctrine, 1918–1939', in Michael Howard
        (ed.). *The theory and practice of war: essays presented to Captain B.H.
        Liddell Hart on his seventieth birthday*. 1965, pp. 187–212.

1137   Gilbert, Felix. 'Two British ambassadors, Perth and Henderson', in Gordon
        Craig and Felix Gilbert (eds.), *The diplomats, 1919–1939*. Princeton,
        N.J., 1953, pp. 537–54. On Perth at Rome and Henderson at Berlin in
        the 1930s.

1138   Gott, Richard. 'The evolution of the independent British deterrent', *Inter-
        national Affairs*, XXXIX (Apr. 1963), 238–52.

1139   Gowen, Robert Joseph. 'Great Britain and the twenty-one demands of
        1915: cooperation versus effacement', *JMH*, XLIII (Mar. 1971), 76–106.

1140   Hall, H. Duncan. 'The genesis of the Balfour Declaration of 1926', *Journal of
        Commonwealth Political Studies*, I (1961–3), 169–93.

1141   Halpern, Paul G. 'The Anglo-French-Italian naval convention of 1915',
        Hist. J., XIII (no. 1, 1970), 106–29.

1142   Hill, Leonidas. 'Three crises, 1938–39', *JCH*, III (Jan. 1968), 113–44.

1143 Johnson, Douglas. 'Austen Chamberlain and the Locarno agreements', *University of Birmingham Historical Journal*, VIII (1961), 62–81.
1144 Joll, James. 'The 1914 debate continues', *PP*, XXXIV (July 1966), pp. 100–13. See comment by Hatton, P.H.S. 'The First World War: Britain and Germany in 1914: the July crisis and war aims', in *PP*, XXXVI (Apr. 1967), 138–43.
1145 Kedourie, Elie. 'The Middle East 1900–1945', in *NCMH*, 269–96.
1146 Kennedy, P.M. 'The development of German naval operations plans against England, 1896–1914', *EHR*, LXXXIX (Jan. 1974), 48–76.
1147 Kernek, Sterling. 'The British Government's reaction to President Wilson's "Peace" note of December 1916', *Hist. J.*, XIII (no. 4, 1970), 721–66.
1148 Klein, Ira. 'Anglo-Russian Convention and the problem of central Asia, 1907–1914', *JBS*, XI (Nov. 1971), 126–47.
1149 —— 'Britain, Siam and the Malay Peninsula 1906–1909', *Hist. J.*, XII (no. 1, 1969), 119–36.
1150 —— 'British intervention in the Persian revolution, 1905–1909', *Hist. J.*, XV (no. 4, 1972), 731–52.
1151 Koch, H.W. 'The Anglo-German alliance negotiations: missed opportunity or myth?', *History*, new ser., LIV (no. 3, 1969), 378–92. On period 1898–1901.
1152 Kurtz, Harold. 'The Lansdowne Letter', *History Today*, XVIII (Feb. 1968), 85–92. Concerning Lansdowne's statement on allied war aims, 30 Nov. 1917.
1153 Lammers, Donald N. 'From Whitehall after Munich: the Foreign Office and the future course of British policy', *Hist. J.*, XVI (no. 4, 1973), 831–56.
1154 —— 'Fascism, Communism, and the Foreign Office, 1937–39', *JCH*, VI (no. 3, 1971), 66–86. Concludes that the Foreign Office had an 'unideological approach'.
1155 Langhorne, Richard. 'Anglo-German negotiations concerning the future of the Portuguese colonies, 1911–1914', *Hist. J.*, XVI (no. 2, 1973), 361–87. For a 'postscript', see J.D. Vincent-Smith in *Hist. J.*, XVII (no. 3, 1974), 620–9.
1156 Larew, Karl G. 'Great Britain and the Greco-Turkish War, 1921–1922', *Historian*, XXXV (Feb. 1973), 256–70.
1157 Louis, William Roger. 'Great Britain and the African Peace Settlement of 1919', *AHR*, LXXI (Apr. 1966), 875–92.
1158 —— 'The United Kingdom and the beginning of the Mandates System, 1919–1922', *International Organization*, XXIII (1969), 73–96. Based on Cabinet Office and Foreign Office papers.
1159 Lovell, Reginald I. 'England is drawn in – July and August, 1914', in Donald C. McKay (ed.), *Essays in the history of modern Europe*. 1936. pp. 149–67. Still useful.
1160 Lowe, Cedric J. 'Britain and Italian intervention 1914–1915', *Hist. J.*, XII (no. 3, 1969), 533–48.
1161 —— 'The failure of British policy in the Balkans, 1914–16', *Canadian Journal of History*, IV (Mar. 1969), 73–100.
1162 Lukowitz, David C. 'British pacifists and appeasement: The Peace Pledge Union', *JCH*, IX (no. 1, 1974), 115–27.
1163 Marder, Arthur J. 'The influence of history on sea power: the Royal Navy and the lessons of 1914–1918', *Pacific Historical Review*, XLI (Nov. 1972), 413–43.
1164 —— 'The royal navy and the Ethiopian crisis of 1935–36', *AHR*, LXXV (June 1970), 1327–56.
1165 Martin, Laurence W. 'Woodrow Wilson's appeals to the people of Europe: British Radical influence on the President's strategy', *Political Science Quarterly*, LXXIV (no. 4, 1959), 498–516.
1166 Murray, John A. 'Foreign policy debated: Sir Edward Grey and his critics, 1911–1912', in Lillian Parker Wallace and William C. Askew (eds.), *Power, public opinion, and diplomacy: essays in honor of Eber Malcolm Carroll*. Durham, N.C., 1959, pp. 140–71.
1167 Nevakivi, Jukka. 'Lord Kitchener and the partition of the Ottoman Empire,

1915–1916', in K. Bourne and Donald Cameron Watt (eds.), *Studies in international history*. 1967, pp. 316–29.

1168 Parker, R.A.C. 'Great Britain, France and the Ethiopian crisis 1935–1936', *EHR*, LXXXIX (Apr. 1974), 293–332.

1169 Penson, Lillian M. *'Obligations by treaty: their place in British foreign policy 1898–1914'*, in Arshag O. Sarkissian (ed.), *Studies in diplomatic history and historiography in honour of G.P. Gooch*. 1961, pp. 76–89.

1170 Pratt, Lawrence. 'The Anglo-American naval conversations on the Far East of January 1938', *International Affairs*, XLVII (Oct. 1971), 745–63.

1171 Renzi, William A. 'Great Britain, Russia and the Straits, 1914–1915', *JMH*, XLII (Mar. 1970), 1–20.

1172 Robbins, Keith. 'British diplomacy and Bulgaria, 1914–1915', *Slavonic and East European Review*, XLIX (Oct. 1971), 560–85.

1173 —— 'Konrad Henlein, the Sudeten question and British foreign policy', *Hist. J.*, XII (no. 4, 1969), 674–97.

1174 Robertson, James C. 'The origins of British opposition to Mussolini over Ethiopia', *JBS*, IX (Nov. 1969), 122–42.

1175 Rock, William R. 'Grand Alliance or daisy chain: British opinion and policy toward Russia, April–August, 1939', in Lillian Parker Wallace and William C. Askew (eds.), *Power, public opinion and diplomacy: essays in honor of Eber Malcolm Carroll*. Durham, N.C., 1959, pp. 297–337.

1176 Rothwell, Victor H. 'Mesopotamia in British war aims, 1914–1918', *Hist. J.*, XIII (no. 2, 1970), 273–94.

1177 Schwoerer, Lois G. 'Lord Halifax's visit to Germany, November 1937', *Historian*, XXXII (May 1970), 353–75.

1178 Scott, William E. 'Neville Chamberlain and Munich: two aspects of power', in Leonard Krieger and Fritz Stern (eds.), *The responsibility of power: historical essays in honor of Hajo Bolborm*. New York, 1967, pp. 353–69.

1179 Smith, C. Jay, Jr. 'Great Britain and the 1914–1915 Straits agreement with Russia: the British promise of November 1914', *AHR*, LXX (July 1965), 1015–34.

1180 Steiner, Zara S. 'Great Britain and the creation of the Anglo-Japanese Alliance', *JMH*, XXXI (Mar. 1959), 27–36.

1181 Steiner, Zara and M.L. Dockrill. 'The Foreign Office reforms, 1919–1921', *Hist. J.*, XVII (no. 1, 1974), 131–56.

1182 Stromberg, Roland N. 'Uncertainties and obscurities about the League of Nations', *JHI*, XXXIII (Jan.–Mar. 1972), 139–54. Includes British contribution to discussion, 1915–1918, of a league or society of nations.

1183 Sweet, David W. 'The Baltic in British diplomacy before the First World War', *Hist. J.*, XIII (no. 3, 1970), 451–90.

1184 Taylor, Alan J.P. 'The war aims of the Allies in the First World War', in his *Politics in wartime*. 1964, pp. 93–122. First published in Richard Pares and A.J.P. Taylor (eds.), *Essays presented to Sir Lewis Namier*. 1956, pp. 475–505.

1185 Toscano, Mario. 'Eden's mission to Rome on the eve of the Italo-Ethiopian conflict', in A.O. Sarkissian (ed.), *Studies in diplomatic history and historiography in honour of G.P. Gooch*. 1961, pp. 126–52.

1186 Vyvyan, J.M.K. 'The approach of the war of 1914', in *NCMH*, 140–70.

1187 Warman, Roberta M. 'The erosion of Foreign Office influence in the making of foreign policy, 1916–18', *Hist. J.*, XV (no. 1, 1972), 133–59.

1188 Watt, Donald Cameron. 'The Anglo-German naval agreement of 1935: an interim judgement', *JMH*, XXVIII (June 1956), 155–75.

1189 —— 'Appeasement: the rise of a revisionist school?', *Political Quarterly*, XXXVI (no. 2, 1965), 191–213. Summarizes the controversy in a manner useful to the general student.

1190 —— 'Diplomatic history 1930–1939', in *NCMH*, 684–734.

1190a Webster, Charles. 'Munich reconsidered: a survey of British policy', *International Affairs*, XXXVII (Apr. 1961), 137–53.

1191 Weinroth, Howard. 'British Radicals and the Agadir Crisis', *European Studies Review*, III (Jan. 1973), 39–61.

1192   —— 'The British Radicals and the balance of power, 1902—1914', *Hist. J.*, XIII (no. 4, 1970), 653—82.

1193   —— 'Left-wing opposition to naval armaments in Britain before 1914', *JCH*, VI (no. 4, 1971), 93—120.

1194   Wells, Samuel F., Jr. 'British strategic withdrawal from the western hemisphere 1904—1906', *Canadian Historical Review*, XLIX (Dec. 1968), 335—56.

1195   Williams, Berl J. 'The strategic background to the Anglo-Russian Entente of August 1907', *Hist. J.*, IX (no. 3, 1966), 360—73.

1196   Wilson, Keith. 'The Agadir crisis, the Mansion House speech, and the double-edgedness of agreements', *Hist. J.*, XV (no. 3, 1972), 513—32.

1197   Winkler, Henry R. 'Arthur Henderson', in Gordon A. Craig and Felix Gilbert (eds.), *The diplomats, 1919—1939*. Princeton, N.J., 1953, pp. 311—43.

1198   —— 'The emergence of a Labour foreign policy in Great Britain, 1918—1929', *JMH*, XXVIII (Sept. 1956), 247—58.

1199   Woodward, David R. 'David Lloyd George, a negotiated peace with Germany, and the Kuhlmann peace kite of September, 1917', *Canadian Journal of History*, VI (Mar. 1971), 75—93.

1200   Woodward, Ernest Llewelyn. 'Diplomatic history of the Second World War', *NCMH*, 798—818.

VII. SOCIAL HISTORY

1 Printed sources
(See also sec. VIII, pt. 1, and sec. XIII, pt. 1, below.)

1201   Beveridge, William. *Social insurance and allied services*. New York, 1942. The famous 'Beveridge plan'.

1202   —— *Power and influence*. 1953. Autobiographical.

1203   Boyd-Orr, John, Baron. *Food health and income; report on a survey of adequacy of diet in relation to income*. 2nd ed., 1937. First issued in 1936. See also Boyd-Orr's autobiography, *As I recall*. 1966.

1204   Brunel, Adrian. *Nice work: the story of thirty years in British film production*. 1949. See also (1271).

1205   Cooper, Lady Diana. *The rainbow comes and goes*. 1958. Continued by *The light of common day*. 1959. Autobiographies.

1206   Fleming Report. *The public schools and the general educational system*. H.M.S.O., 1944. Report of a committee headed by Lord Fleming, appointed by the president of the Board of Education.

1207   Gosden, Peter H.J.H. (ed.). *How they were taught: an anthology of contemporary accounts of learning and teaching in England, 1880—1950*. New York, 1969.

1208   Jones, Kathleen (ed.). *The Year Book of Social Policy in Britain, 1971—*. 1972—. An annual publication, discussing the issues of the year covered; the latest volume is for 1973 (1974).

1209   Laver, James. *Edwardian promenade*. Boston, Mass., 1958. Selections from contemporary material.

1210   Lehmann, John. *I am my brother*. New York, 1960. Autobiographical; life in London 1939—45, by a man of letters.

1211   Lester, Muriel. *It occurred to me*. 1937. Autobiographical account of the life of a social and religious worker.

1212   Lubbock, Percy. *Earlham*. 1963. Fascinating account of country life of upper classes in early 1900s. First published 1922.

1213   Lunn, Arnold. *Memory to memory*. 1956. Autobiography of a well-known mountaineer.

1214   *Mass-observation*. See Madge, Charles and Tom Harrison, *Mass-observation*. 1937. An introduction to the series. Publications include: *Puzzled people: a study in popular attitudes to religion, ethics, progress and politics in a*

London borough (1947); The pub and the people: a work—town study (Welwyn-Garden City, 1970).

1215 Masterman, Charles F.G. *The condition of England*, ed. James T. Boulton. 1960. First published in 1909. A significant analysis of Edwardian society.

1216 —— *England after war: a study*. New York, 1923. A contemporary view, widely read.

1217 Mitchell, Hannah. *The hard way up: the autobiography of Hannah Mitchell, suffragette and rebel*, ed. Geoffrey Mitchell. 1968.

1218 Morrell, Lady Ottoline. *Memoirs of Lady Ottoline Morrell: a study in friendship 1873—1915*, ed. Robert Gathorne-Hardy. New York, 1964. Continued by *Ottoline at Garsington*. 1974. Memoirs carried to 1918 with later comment by Lady Ottoline.

1219 Nettleingham, Frederick T. *Tommy's tunes*. 1917. Soldier songs during World War I.

1220 Newsholme, Arthur. *The last thirty years in public health: recollections and reflections on my official and post-official life*, 1936. Newsholme was principal medical officer with the Local Government Board, 1908—19.

1221 The Newsom Report. *The Public Schools Commission first report*. 1966. Concerns 'independent day schools and direct grant grammar schools'. See also *The Public Schools Commission second report* (known as the 'Donnison Report'). 1970, 3 vols.

1222 O'Neill, William L. *The woman movement: feminism in the United States and England*. 1969. Documents with commentary.

1223 Padley, Richard and Margaret Cole (eds.). *Evacuation survey: a report to the Fabian Society*. 1940. Valuable accounts of evacuation from London, 1939.

1224 Pankhurst, E. Sylvia. *The Suffragette movement: an intimate account of persons and ideals*. 1931.

1225 Pike, E. Royston (ed.). *'Busy times': human documents of the age of the Forsytes*. 1969.

1226 Plowden Report. *Children and their primary schools: a report of the central advisory council for education (England)*. 1967, 2 vols. Lady Plowden was chairman of the council.

1227 Priestley, John B. *Britain speaks*. New York, 1940. English edition, *Postscripts*. 1940. Broadcasts, May—September, 1940.

1228 —— *English journey*. 1934. An account of a journey in autumn of 1933.

1229 Read, Donald (ed.). *Documents from Edwardian England 1901—1915*. 1973.

1230 Reith, John Charles Walsham, Baron. *Into the wind*. 1949. Autobiography of the Director General of the BBC, 1927—38.

1231 Rowntree, B. Seebohm and George R. Lavers. *English life and leisure: a social study*. 1951. Case histories.

1232 *Royal commission on population*. Cmd. Report 7695. 1949. Repr., 1953.

1233 Swanwick, Helena M.L. *I have been young*. 1935. Autobiography.

1234 —— *The war and its effect upon women* and *Women and war*. 1971. Reprint of World War pamphlets.

1235 Tawney, Richard H. *The acquisitive society*. 1921. First published (1920) as *The sickness of an acquisitive society*. A celebrated tract of the times.

1236 Titmuss, Richard M. *Poverty and population: a factual study of contemporary social waste*. 1938.

2 Surveys

1237 Borer, Mary Cathcart. *Britain — twentieth century: the story of social conditions*. 1967.

1238 Branson, Noreen and Margot Heinemann. *Britain in the nineteen thirties*. 1971. This book has been described 'as a product of the unreconstructed left'.

1239 Carr-Saunders, Alexander M. and D. Caradog Jones and Claus A. Moser. *A survey of social conditions in England and Wales as illustrated by statistics*. 3rd ed., Oxford, 1958. Cf. 1st ed. (1927), published as *A survey of the social structure of England and Wales*.

1240 Graves, Robert and Alan Hodge. *The long week-end: a social history of Great Britain 1918—1939*. 1940. Written with knowledge and spirit.

1241 Gregg, Pauline. *A social and economic history of Britain 1760—1972*. 7th ed., rev., 1973.

1242 —— *The welfare state: an economic and social history of Great Britain from 1945 to the present day*. 1967.

1243 Halsey, Albert H. (ed.). *Trends in British society since 1900: a guide to the changing social structure of Britain*. 1972. Sixteen scholarly and informative articles.

1244 Hearnshaw, Fossey J.C. (ed.). *Edwardian England, A.D. 1900—1910*. 1933. As seen by scholars forty years ago.

1245 Hopkins, Harry. *The new look: a social history of the forties and fifties in Britain*. 1963.

1246 Johns, Edward A. *The social structure of modern Britain*. 2nd ed., 1972. An excellent introduction.

1247 Macqueen-Pope, Walter J. *Twenty shillings in the pound*. 1948. Popular account of life in Edwardian Britain.

1248 Marsh, David Charles. *The changing social structure of England and Wales 1871—1961*. Rev. ed., 1965.

1249 Marwick, Arthur J.B. *Britain in the century of total war: war, peace and social change, 1900—1967*. 1968. See also Marwick, *The explosion of British society, 1914—62*. 1963.

1250 Montgomery, John. *The twenties: an informal social history*. 1957.

1251 —— *The fifties*. 1965.

1252 Muggeridge, Malcolm. *The sun never sets: the story of England in the nineteen-thirties*. New York, 1940. English edition as, *The Thirties: 1930—1940 in Great Britain*. 1940.

1253 Nowell-Smith, Simon (ed.). *Edwardian England 1901—1914*. 1964. Well informed articles, presented in popular style.

1254 Ogilvie, Vivian. *Our times: a social history, 1912—1952*. 1953.

1255 Read, Donald. *Edwardian England 1901—1915: society and politics*. 1972. One of the best books on the period.

1256 —— *The English provinces: c. 1760—1960: a study in influence*. 1964. Includes extensive treatment of the relation of the provinces to the London area in the twentieth century.

1257 Roebuck, Janet. *The making of modern English society from 1850*. 1973. Includes an excellent bibliography.

1258 Ryder, Judith and Harold Silver. *Modern English society: history and structure 1850—1970*. 1970.

1259 Seaman, Lewis C.B. *Life in Britain between the wars*. 1970. Popular account, informative.

1260 Williams, Thomas G. *The main currents of social and industrial change 1870—1924*. 1925.

3 Monographs
(See also sec. VIII, pt. 3, and sec. XIII, pt. 3, below.)

1261 Abbott, Albert. *Education for industry and commerce in England*. 1933. Extensive and reliable survey of technical education before 1933.

1262 Abel-Smith, Brian. *A history of the nursing profession*. 1960.

1263 —— *The hospitals, 1800—1948: a study in social administration in England and Wales*. Cambridge, Mass., 1964. Largely on the twentieth century.

1264 Abrams, Mark. *The population of Great Britain: current trends and future problems*. 1945.

1265 Atkinson, Anthony B. *Poverty in Britain and the reform of social security*. Cambridge, 1969.

1266 Bagley, John J. and A.J. *The state and education in England and Wales, 1833—1968*. 1969. Brief general treatment, well done.

1267 Banks, Olive. *Parity and prestige in English secondary education*. 1955.

1268 Bell, E. Moberly. *Storming the citadel: the rise of the woman doctor*. 1953.

1269   Benjamin, Bernard. *The population census*. 1970. Sponsored by the Social
        Science Research Council; a brief, useful analysis.
1270   Bernbaum, Gerald. *Social change and the schools, 1918—1944*. 1967.
1271   Betts, Ernest. *The film business: a history of British cinema 1896—1972*.
        1973. The best account. See also (1204).
1272   Beveridge, William H. *The London School of Economics and its problems
        1919—1937*. 1960.
1273   Blyth, William A.L. *English primary education: a sociological description*.
        1965, 2 vols. Vol. I provides historical background.
1274   Blythe, Ronald. *Akenfield: portrait of an English village*. New York, 1969.
        Absorbing sociological study.
1275   Bogdanor, Vernon and Robert Skidelsky (eds.). *Age of affluence 1951—1964*.
        1970. Essays by various writers.
1276   Bonham-Carter, Victor. *Dartington Hall, the history of an experiment*. 1958.
        A story of economic and social rehabilitation as well as of an educational
        enterprize.
1277   Booker, Christopher. *The Neophiliacs*. 1969. Its theme is 'the psychic epi-
        demic' of the fifties and sixties.
1278   Bowley, Arthur L. and Margaret H. Hogg. *Has poverty diminished?* 1925.
        Based on a study made in 1924.
1279   Bowley, Marian. *Housing and the state, 1919—1944*. 1945. Still standard.
1280   Bramwell, Robert D. *Elementary school work 1900—1925*. Durham, 1961.
1281   Briggs, Asa. *Mass entertainment; the origins of a modern industry*. Adelaide,
        1960. A lecture.
1282   —— *The history of broadcasting in the United Kingdom*. 1961—70, 3 vols.
        Takes the story to 1945.
1283   Brittain, Vera. *Lady into woman: a history of women from Victoria to
        Elizabeth II*. 1953. Largely on the twentieth century.
1284   Brockington, C. Fraser. *A short history of public health*. 2nd ed., 1966.
1285   Brooke, Iris. *English costume 1900—1950*. 1951.
1286   Buchanan, Colin D. *Mixed blessing: the motor in Britain*. 1958.
1287   Buchanan Colin M. *The state of Britain*. 1972. The Chichele lectures at
        Oxford in 1971; a neat summary of the history of planning measures.
1288   Burnett, John. *Plenty and want: a social history of diet in England from 1815
        to the present day*. 1966.
1289   Calder, Angus. *The people's war: Britain 1939—45*. 1969. Very informative,
        though not always reliable. Excellent bibliography.
1290   Clark, Ronald W. and Edward C. Pyatt. *Mountaineering in Britain: a history
        from the earliest times to the present day*. 1957.
1291   Coates, R.D. *Teachers' Unions and interest group politics: a study in the be-
        haviour of organised teachers in England and Wales*. Cambridge, 1972.
        Detailed examination of the sixties.
1292   Cole, George D.H. and M.I. *The condition of Britain*. 1937. The tables are
        particularly useful.
1293   Cole, George D.H. *The post-war condition of Britain*. 1956. Much infor-
        mation, but somewhat ill-digested.
1294   —— *A short history of the British working-class movement, 1789—1947*.
        2nd ed., 1948. Half of it on twentieth century.
1295   —— *Studies in class structure*. 1955. Of the six 'studies', four are reprints.
1296   Cunnington, C. Willett. *English women's clothing in the present century*.
        1952. An excellent work, well illustrated.
1297   Curtis, Stanley J. *Education in Britain since 1900*. 1952. More useful on
        twentieth century than his excellent *History of education in Great Britain*.
        7th ed., 1967.
1298   Dent, Harold Collett. *The educational system of England and Wales*. 1961.
1299   —— *1870—1970: century of growth in English education*. 1970.
1300   —— *Growth in English education 1946—1952*. 1954. The best work on the
        subject.
1301   Eckstein, Harry. *The English health service: its origins, structure and achieve-
        ments*. 1958. One of the most satisfactory works on the subject.

1302   Ferguson, Sheila and Hilde Fitzgerald. *Studies in the social services*. 1954. Successor to R.M. Titmuss, *Problems of Social policy*. 1950.
1303   Ford, Percy. *Social theory and social practice: an exploration of experience*. Shannon, 1968. Efforts in the nineteenth and twentieth centuries at social planning as found in parliamentary reports.
1304   Forrest, Denys. *Tea for the British: the social and economic history of a famous trade*. 1973.
1305   Garrard, John A. *The English and immigration, 1880—1910*. 1971. A study of opinion on East European immigration into Britain.
1306   Gemmill, Paul F. *Britain's search for health: the first twelve years of the National Health Service*. Philadelphia, 1962.
1307   George, V. *Social security: Beveridge and after*. 1968. Detailed analysis of income maintenance since 1945.
1308   Glass, David V. *Population policies and movements in Europe*. 1940. Includes an extensive and suggestive analysis of experience in England and Wales, with useful references.
1309   —— (ed.). *Social mobility in Britain*. Glencoe, Illinois, 1954. Fourteen articles by various authors.
1310   Gorham, Maurice. *Broadcasting and television since 1900*. 1952.
1311   Gosden, Peter H.J.H. *The development of educational administration in England and Wales*. Oxford, 1966.
1312   Gosling, John and Dennis Craig. *The great train robbery*. 1964. Popular account of a well-known event, 8 Aug. 1963.
1313   Graves, John. *Policy and progress in secondary education, 1902—1942*. 1943.
1314   Hall, M. Penelope. *The social services of modern England*. 6th ed., 1963.
1315   Harris, Richard W. *National health insurance in Great Britain, 1911—1946*. 1946.
1316   Hartley, A. *A state of Britain*. 1963.
1317   Hiro, Dilip. *Black British white British*. 1971. Thorough but not as good as (1351).
1318   Hoggart, Richard. *The uses of literacy: aspects of working-class life, with special reference to publications and entertainments*. 1957. Significant study of changes in working-class culture since World War I.
1319   Hubback, Eva M. *The population of Britain*. 1947. A general treatment, well presented, partly historical, partly contemporary comment.
1320   Isaac, Julius. *British post-war migration*. Cambridge, 1954.
1321   Jenkins, Inez. *History of the Women's Institute Movement of England and Wales*. 1953.
1322   Jones, Kathleen. *Mental health and social policy, 1845—1959*. 1960.
1323   Kazamias, Andreas M. *Politics, society and secondary education in England*. Philadelphia, 1966. Sets out 'to interpret educational events [since 1895] in their *historical* context'.
1324   Klein, Viola. *Britain's married women workers*. 1965. An historical and sociological study; includes statistical data.
1325   Lees-Milne, James. *Britain's heritage: a record of the National Trust*. 2nd ed., 1948.
1326   Lester-Smith, W.O. *Education in Great Britain*. 5th ed., 1967. General account of developments since 1944.
1327   Lewis, Roy and Angus Maude. *The English middle classes*. 1949. Historical context.
1328   —— *Professional people*. 1952.
1329   Lindsey, Almont. *Socialized medicine in England and Wales: the National Health Service 1948—1961*. Chapel Hill, N.C., 1962.
1330   Lipman, Vivian D. *Social history of the Jews in England, 1850—1950*. 1954.
1331   Low, Rachel. *The history of the British film*. 1948—1971, 4 vols.
1332   Lowndes, George A.N. *The silent social revolution: an account of the expansion of public education in England and Wales, 1895—1965*. 2nd ed., 1969. One of the best surveys.
1333   McGregor, Oliver R. *Divorce in England: a centenary study*. 1957. Scholarly.
1334   Mack, Edward C. *Public schools and British opinion since 1860*. New York, 1941. Emphasis upon developments in twentieth century.

1335   Marples, Morris. *A history of football*. 1954. Well informed, well documented.
1336   Marsh, David Charles. *The welfare state*. 1970. A good introduction.
1337   Marshall, Thomas H. *Social policy in the twentieth century*. 2nd ed., 1967.
1338   Marwick, Arthur J.B. *The deluge: British society and the First World War*. 1965. See also his 'The impact of the First World War on British Society', *JCH*, III (Jan. 1968), 51—63.
1339   Mendelsohn, Ronald. *Social security in the British Commonwealth: Great Britain, Canada, Australia, New Zealand*. 1954. Useful comparative study.
1340   Mess, Henry Adolphis. *Voluntary social services since 1918*, ed. Gertrude Williams. [1948.]
1341   Mitchell, David J. *Women on the warpath: the story of the women of the First World War*. 1966. First published (1965) as *Monstrous Regiment*.
1342   —— *The fighting Pankhursts: a study in tenacity*. 1967. Concerns Emmeline, Christabel, Sylvia and Adela Pankhurst.
1343   Montgomery, Robert J. *Examinations: an account of their evolution as administrative devices in England*. 1965.
1344   Moore, John. *Portrait of Elmbury*. 1945. Between the wars; 'Elmbury' is really Tewkesbury.
1345   Mosley, Leonard. *Backs to the wall: London under fire 1939—45*. 1971. Popular.
1346   Murphy, James. *Church, state and schools in Britain, 1890—1970*. 1971.
1347   Newton, Kenneth. *The sociology of British communism*. 1969. In a historical context.
1348   Palmer, Cecil. *The British Socialist ill-fare state*. 1952. A hostile view.
1349   Parkin, Frank. *Middle class radicalism: the social bases of the British campaign for nuclear disarmament*. Manchester, 1968.
1350   Parkinson, Michael. *The Labour Party and the organization of secondary education 1918—1965*. 1970.
1351   Patterson, Sheila. *Immigration and race relations in Britain 1960—1967*. 1969. The best treatment.
1352   Pelling, Henry. *Britain and the Second World War*. 1970. Good brief account. Cf. Longmate, Norman. *The way we lived then: a history of every-day life during the Second World War*. 1971.
1353   Pinchbeck, Ivy and Margaret Hewitt. *Children in English society*, II, *From the eighteenth century to the Children Act, 1948*. 1973.
1354   Playne, Caroline E. *Society at war 1914—1916*. 1931. Continued by her *Britain holds on 1917—1918*. 1933.
1355   —— *The pre-war mind in Britain*. 1928. A popular but sensitive analysis of the mentality of British society.
1356   Prain, Eric (ed.). *The Oxford and Cambridge Golfing Society, 1898—1948*. 1949. Chapters by various authors; includes results of matches.
1357   Rodgers, Brian. *The battle against poverty*. 1968—9, 2 vols. 'A short text'.
1358   Rose, Eliot J.B. *et al. Colour and citizenship: a report on British race relations*. 1969. Sponsored by the Institute of Race Relations; an excellent analysis in a historical setting.
1359   Rose, Hilary and Steven. *Science and society*. 1969. Interrelations of science, technology and society in the twentieth century.
1360   Ross, James Stirling. *The National Health Service in Great Britain: an historical and descriptive study*. 1952.
1361   Rubenstein, David and Brian Simon. *The evolution of the comprehensive school, 1926—1966*. 1969.
1362   Runciman, Walter G. *Relative deprivation and social justice: a study of attitudes to social inequality in twentieth-century England*. Berkeley, Cal., 1966.
1363   Sampson, Anthony. *Anatomy of Britain*. 1962. A new and enlarged edition, *Anatomy of Britain today*. 1965. Examination of contemporary politics and society in an historical context.
1364   Saran, Rene. *Policy-making in secondary education: a case study*. Oxford, 1973. A study of a large urbanized county in south of England, 1944—64.
1365   Selleck, Richard J.W. *English primary education and the progressives, 1914—1939*. 1972.

1366   Shulman, Milton. *The least worst television in the world*. 1973. 'Personal survey' of the sixties and seventies.
1367   Simon, Brian. *Studies in the History of Education*, II, *Education and the labour movement, 1870–1920*, 1960. III, *The politics of educational reform, 1920–1940*, 1974.
1368   Sissons, Michael and Philip French (eds.). *Age of austerity*. 1963. Essays on post-war Britain by writers too young to vote in 1945.
1369   Stocks, Mary. *The Workers' Educational Association: the first fifty years*. 1953.
1370   Strachey, Ray. *'The Cause': a short history of the women's movement in Great Britain*. 1928.
1371   Titmuss, Richard and Kathleen. *Parents revolt: a study of the declining birthrate in acquisitive societies*. 1942.
1372   Titmuss, Richard. *Essays on the 'Welfare State'*. 2nd ed., 1963. Lectures and essays, some of them reprints, by a leading social scientist.
1373   —— *Income distribution and social change*. 1962. In a historical context.
1374   Trow-Smith, Robert. *Society and the land*. 1952. Discussion of the relations of society, farm land and farm people.
1375   Turner, Ernest S. *What the butler saw: two hundred and fifty years of the servant problem*. 1962. Carries the story to about 1945.
1376   Vaizey, John. *The costs of education*. 1958. Based on historical data fully provided.
1377   Wardle, David. *English popular education 1780–1970*. Cambridge, 1970. Includes a summary of developments in the twentieth century.
1378   Wickwar, Hardy and Margaret. *The social services: an historical survey*. Rev. ed., 1949.
1379   Wilson, H.H. *Pressure group: the campaign for commercial television in England*. New Brunswick, N.J., 1961.
1380   Worsfold, W. Basil. *The war and social reform*. 1919. 'An endeavour to trace the influence of the war as a reforming agency'.
1381   Young, Agnes F. *Social services in British industry*. 1968. Largely, developments after 1945.

4 Biographies

1382   Beveridge, Janet. *Beveridge and his plan*. 1954.
1383   Boardman, Philip. *Patrick Geddes: maker of the future*. Chapel Hill, N.C., 1944. Biography of a biologist, sociologist, educationist and town planner.
1384   Briggs, Asa. *Social thought and social action, a study of the work of Seebohm Rowntree 1871–1954*. 1961.
1385   Hillcourt, William. *Baden-Powell: the two lives of a hero*. 1964. 'Life Number Two' was with the Boy Scout movement.
1386   Mansbridge, Albert. *Margaret McMillan, prophet and pioneer: her life and work*. 1932.
1387   Martin, Ralph G. *Jennie: the life of Lady Randolph Churchill*. Englewood Cliffs, N.J., 1969–71, 2 vols. A documented life, in popular style, of the mother of Winston Churchill.
1388   Stocks, Mary. *Eleanor Rathbone: a biography*. 1949. Useful examination of the life of a social worker and member of parliament.
1389   Wood, Alan. *Mr Rank: a study of J. Arthur Rank and British films*. 1952.

5 Articles
(See also sec. VIII, pt. 5, and sec. XIII, pt. 5, below.)

1390   Abrams, Philip. 'The failure of social reform: 1918–1920', *PP*, XXIV (Apr. 1963), 43–64.
1391   Akenson, D.H. 'Patterns of English educational change: the Fisher and the Butler Acts', *History of Education Quarterly*, XI (Summer 1971), 143–56.
1392   Becker, Arthur Peter. 'Housing in England and Wales during the business depression of the 1930s', *EcHR*, 2nd ser., III (1950–1), 321–41.

1393   Bonnor, John. 'The four Labour cabinets', *Sociological Review*, new ser., VI
       (July 1958), 37—48. A study of social origins, education and occupation.
1394   Bowley, Marian. 'The housing statistics of Great Britain', *Journal of the Royal
       Statistical Society*, CXIII (1950), 396—411. On the period 1861—1938.
1395   Briggs, Asa. 'The welfare state in historical perspective', *Archives Européenes
       de Sociologie*, II (no. 2, 1961), 221—58. An excellent commentary.
1396   Dean, D.W. 'Conservatism and the national education system 1922—40', *JCH*,
       VI (no. 2, 1971), 150—65.
1397   ——— 'The difficulties of a Labour educational policy: the failure of the
       Trevelyan Bill, 1929—1931', *BJES*, XVII (Oct. 1969), 286—300.
1398   ——— 'H.A.L. Fisher, reconstruction and the development of the 1918 Edu-
       cation Act', *BJES*, XVIII (Oct. 1970), 259—76.
1399   Dingle, A.E. 'Drink and working-class living standards in Britain, 1870—1914',
       EcHR, 2nd ser., XXV (no. 4, 1972), 608—21.
1400   Eaglesham, Eric. 'Implementing the Education Act of 1902', *BJES*, X (1961—
       2), 153—75.
1401   ——— 'Planning the Education Bill of 1902', *BJES*, IX (Nov. 1960), 3—24.
1402   Friedlander, D. and R.J. Roshier. 'A study of internal migration in England
       and Wales: Part I', *Population Studies*, XIX (Mar. 1956), 239—79. On the
       period 1851—1951.
1403   Gillis, John R. 'Conformity and rebellion: contrasting styles of English and
       German youth, 1900—1933', *History of Education Quarterly*, XIII (Fall
       1973), 249—60.
1404   Greenwood, Major. 'British loss of life in the wars of 1794—1815 and in
       1914—1918', *Journal of the Royal Statistical Society*, CV (pt. I, 1942),
       1—16.
1405   Harbury, C.D. and P.C. McMahon. 'Inheritance and the characteristics of top
       wealth leavers in Britain', *EJ*, LXXXIII (Sept. 1973), 810—33.
1406   Jenkins, E.W. 'The Thomson Committee and the Board of Education 1916—
       1922', *BJES*, XXI (Feb. 1973), 76—87. Concerning the position of
       Natural Science in the educational system.
1407   Krausz, Ernest. 'Factors of social mobility in British minority groups', *BJS*,
       XXIII (Sept. 1972), 275—86.
1408   Lamb, H.H. 'Britain's changing climate', *GJ*, CXXXIII (Dec. 1967), 445—68.
1409   Lepmann, Kaethe K. 'English housing policy since the war', *American Econ-
       omic Review*, XXVII (Sept. 1937), 503—18.
1410   MacDougall. G.D.A. 'Inter-war population changes in town and country',
       Journal of the Royal Statistical Society, CIII (1940), 30—60. 'A paper'
       with critical comments.
1411   McGregor, Oliver R. 'The Morton Commission: a social and historical com-
       mentary', *BJS*, VII (1956), 171—93. Concerning the report of the Royal
       Commission on Marriage and Divorce (1956).
1412   Marwick, Arthur J.B. 'British life and leisure and the First World War', *His-
       tory Today*, XV (June 1965), 409—19.
1413   Middleton, Nigel. 'Lord Butler and the Education Act of 1944', *BJES*, XX
       (June 1972), 178—91.
1414   Morgan, John S. 'The break-up of the poor law in Britain, 1907—47: an his-
       torical footnote', *Canadian Journal of Economics and Political Science*,
       XIV (May 1948), 209—19. An analysis of social legislation.
1415   Pierce, Rachel M. 'Marriage in the fifties', *Sociological Review*, new ser., II
       (July 1963), 215—40. Based on inquiry into changing marriage habits.
1416   Reid, F. 'Socialist Sunday Schools in Great Britain 1892—1939', *IRSH*, XI
       (pt. 1, 1966), 18—46.
1417   Rogers, Alan. 'Churches and children — a study in the controversy over the
       1902 Education Act', *BJES*, VIII (Nov. 1959), 29—51.
1418   Springhall, J.O. 'The Boy Scouts, class and militarism in relation to British
       youth movements, 1908—1930', *IRSH*, XVI (pt. 2, 1971), 125—58.
1419   Usherwood, Stephen. 'The B.B.C. and the General Strike', *History Today*,
       XXII (Dec. 1972), 858—65. Popular account, with interesting detail.
1420   Whitfield, George. 'The grammar schools through half a century', *BJES*, V
       (May 1957), 101—18. By a headmaster of Hampton Grammar School.

1421   Wilkinson, Paul. 'English youth movements, 1908–30', *JCH*, IV (Apr. 1969), 3–23.
1422   Willatts, E.C. and Marion G.C. Newson. 'The geographical pattern of population changes in England and Wales, 1921–1951', *GJ*, CXIX (Dec. 1953), 431–54.
1423   Wilson, J. 'British Israelism', *Sociological Review*, new ser., XVI (Mar. 1968), 41–57. As an organized element.

VIII. ECONOMIC HISTORY

1 Printed sources

1424   Arnot, R. Page. *The general strike, May 1926: its origin and history*. Reprint, 1967. Originally published by the Labour Research Department, 1926. Useful documentary account, with comment.
1425   Beales, H.L. and R.S. Lambert (eds.). *Memoirs of the unemployed*. 1934. Originally published in *The Listener*, 1933.
1426   Beveridge, William H. *Full employment in a free society*. New York, 1945. Reflects Keynesian influence; includes an appendix on economic fluctuations.
1427   —— *Unemployment: a problem of industry*. 2nd ed., 1910. Based on lectures at Oxford in 1908.
1428   Brown, William J. *So far . . .* 1943. Autobiography of a journalist, trade union adviser and Labour M.P.
1429   Burns, Emile. *The General Strike, May 1926: trades councils in action*. (Labour Research Department) 1926. Concerning local strike organisation.
1430   Chiozza Money, Leo G. *Riches and poverty*. 1905. A classic statement.
1431   Citrine, Walter McLennan, Baron. *An autobiography*. 1964–7, 2 vols. By the general-secretary of the T.U.C., 1926–46.
1432   Coates, Ken and Anthony Tophan. *Industrial democracy in Great Britain*. 1968. A book of readings.
1433   Drummond, Ian M. *British economic policy and the empire, 1919–1939*. 1972. Documents with commentary.
1434   *The General Strike: the British gazette and the British worker*. Reprints of issues for 5 May to 13 May 1926 of the Government paper and the Trades Union Congress paper.
1435   Glasgow, George. *General strikes and road transport*. [1926.]
1436   Gleason, Arthur. *What the workers want: a study of British labour*. New York, 1920. See also Kellogg, Paul U. and Arthur Gleason, *British labor and the war: reconstructors for a new world*. New York, 1919.
1437   Greenwood, Walter. *Love on the dole*. New ed., 1955. Originally published in 1933, this novel accurately depicts 'depressed areas'.
1438   Hannington, Wal. *Unemployed struggles 1919–1936: my life and struggles amongst the unemployed*. 1936. Hannington's other books include *Ten lean years: an examination of the record of the National Government in the field of unemployment*. 1940.
1439   Harrison, Norman. *Once a miner*. 1954. Personal experience in the 1940s.
1440   Hilton, John. *Rich man, poor man*. 1944. Absorbing treatment of the 'unequal distribution of wealth'.
1441   Keynes, John Maynard. *Collected writings*, ed. Donald E. Moggridge. 1971–. In progress; ten of projected 24 volumes had been published by the end of 1973.
1442   —— *The General Theory of employment, interest and money*. 1936. Not yet in (1441).
1443   Lane, Peter (ed.). *Documents on British economic and social policy*. II, *1870–1939*, 1968. III, *1945–1967*, 1969. An excellent collection.
1444   Leeson, Robert A. *Strike: a live history 1887–1971*. 1973. 'Recollections of some 80 people in some 180 strikes'.
1445   Macmillan, Harold. *The middle way: a study of the problem of economic*

and social progress in a free and democratic society. 1938. Revealing on both author and subject.

1446 Mantoux, Étienne. *The Carthaginian Peace, or the economic consequences of Mr Keynes.* 1946. An answer to John Maynard Keynes, *The Economic consequences of the peace,* in (1441).

1447 Markham, Violet R. *Return passage.* 1953. Autobiography of a leading member of the Unemployment Assistance Board created in 1934.

1448 *Men without work: a report made to the Pilgrim Trust.* Cambridge, 1938. A social analysis of the unemployed in the thirties.

1449 *The National Plan.* 1965. Drafted by the British National Economic Development Council and presented to parliament, September 1965.

1450 *Oxford pamphlets 1914—1915.* N.d. War-time statements on the economy, showing how problems looked then.

1451 Pearson, Arthur J. *Man of the rail.* 1967. A personal account by a practitioner of technical journalism.

1452 *Report of the . . . annual Trades Union Congress,* 1901–. Manchester, 1901–.

1453 Robbins, Lionel Charles, Baron. *Autobiography of an economist.* 1971.

1454 Robertson, Norman and Kenneth I. Sams. *British trade unionism: select documents.* Oxford, 1972, 2 vols. Useful work of reference.

1455 Rolt, Lionel T.C. *Landscape with machines: an autobiography.* 1971. By a noted author of railroad history.

1456 *Royal Commission on trade unions and employers' associations 1965—1968: report presented . . . June 1968.* [1968]. Cmnd 3623. Known as the 'Donovan Report'.

1457 Salter, Arthur. *Recovery: the second effort.* 1932. By a noted scholar and statesman.

1458 [Stewart, Robert]. *Breaking the fetters: the memoirs of Bob Stewart.* 1967. A story, carried to about 1930, by an active worker in Scottish trade unionism and communism.

1459 Sturt, George. *The journals of George Sturt 1890—1927,* ed. Eric D. Mackerness. 1967, 2 vols. Sturt (1863—1927) was associated with the wheelwright craft and industry.

2 Surveys
(See also sec. VII, pt. 2, above.)

1460 Abrams, Mark. *The condition of the British people 1911—1945: a study prepared for the Fabian Society.* 1946. Statistical.

1461 Aldcroft, Derek H. *The inter-war economy: Britain, 1919—1939.* 1970. Best work on the period.

1462 Aldcroft, Derek H. and Harry W. Richardson. *The British economy, 1870—1939.* 1969. An introduction to the central themes and problems with invaluable bibliography.

1463 Ashworth, William. *An economic history of England 1870—1939.* 1960. A comprehensive survey.

1464 Bagwell, Philip S. and G.E. Mingay. *Britain and America 1850—1939: a study of economic change.* 1970. A comparative study.

1465 Clapham, John H. *An economic history of modern Britain.* III: *Machines and national rivalries (1887—1914) with an epilogue (1914—1929).* Cambridge, 1938. Rather thin after 1914.

1466 Dunning, John H. and C.J. Thomas. *British industry: change and development in the twentieth century.* 1961.

1467 Hobsbawm, Eric J. *Industry and empire: the making of modern English society.* II: *1750 to the present day.* 1968.

1468 Johnson, Walford *et al. A short economic and social history of twentieth-century Britain.* 1967. Excellent brief account.

1469 Jones, Gwilym and A.G. Pool. *A hundred years of economic development in Great Britain.* 1940. Carries story to 1939.

1470 Lewis, W. Arthur. *Economic survey 1919—1939.* 1949. Perhaps the best introduction to international aspects.

ECONOMIC HISTORY

1471 McDonnell, K.G.T. *et al. A survey of English economic history*, ed. Maurice W. Thomas. 2nd ed., 1960.
1472 Mathias, Peter. *The first industrial nation: an economic history of Britain, 1700–1914.* 1969. Good up-to-date treatment of period 1870–1914.
1473 Phillips, G.A. and R.T. Maddock. *The growth of the British economy 1918–1968.* 1973.
1474 Pollard, Sidney. *The development of the British economy, 1914–1967.* 2nd ed., 1969. Excellent.
1475 Sayers, Richard S. *A history of economic change in England 1880–1939.* 1967.
1476 Shonfield, Andrew. *British economic policy since the war.* 1958.
1477 Smith, Wilfred. *An economic geography of Great Britain.* 2nd ed., 1953. Part I is historical and Part II is 'Present economic geography'.
1478 Youngson, Alexander J. *Britain's economic growth 1920–1966.* 1967. An extension of his *The British Economy, 1920–1957.* 1960.

3 Monographs
(See also sec. VII, pt. 3 above and sec. IX, pt. 3, below.)

1479 Abel, Deryck. *A history of British tariffs 1923–1942.* 1945.
1480 Abel-Smith, Brian and Richard M. Titmuss. *The cost of the national health service in England and Wales.* Cambridge, 1956.
1481 Aldcroft, Derek H. *British railways in transition: the economic problems of Britain's railways since 1914.* 1968.
1482 Aldcroft, Derek H. and Peter Fearon (eds.). *Economic growth in twentieth-century Britain.* 1969. Thirteen articles by recognized scholars.
1483 Alexander, Kenneth J.W. and C.L. Jenkins. *Fairfields: a study of industrial change.* 1970. Study of the ship building industry.
1484 Alford, B.W.E. *W.D. & H.O. Wills and the development of the U.K. tobacco industry 1786–1965.* 1973.
1485 Allen, Cecil J. *Locomotive practice and performance in the twentieth century.* Cambridge, 1949.
1486 Allen, George C. *British industries and their organization.* 4th ed., 1959.
1487 ——— *The structure of industry in Britain: a study in economic change.* 1961. On 1900–60.
1488 Allen, Victor L. *Trade union leadership, based on a study of Arthur Deakin.* 1957. Deakin was general secretary of the Transport and General Workers Union — its history after 1940 is examined in detail.
1489 ——— *Trade unions and the government.* 1960.
1490 Amulree, William Warrender MacKenzie, 1st Baron. *Industrial arbitration in Great Britain.* 1929. Excellent account, representative of its time.
1491 Anderson, Adelaide Mary. *Women in the factory.* New York, 1922. Story of the Woman Inspectorate of Factories and Workshops, 1893–1921.
1492 Anderson, John R.L. *East of Suez: a study of Britain's greatest trading enterprise.* 1969. Story of British petroleum from 1909.
1493 Andréadès, Andreas. *Philip Snowden: the man and his financial policy.* 1930.
1494 Andrews, Irene Osgood. *Economic effects of the war upon women and children in Great Britain.* New York, 1918.
1495 Andrews, Philip W.S. and Elizabeth Brunner. *Capital development in steel: a study of the United Steel Companies Ltd.* Oxford, 1951.
1496 Arndt, Heinz W. *The economic lessons of the nineteen-thirties.* 1944.
1497 Arnot, R. Page. *The Miners: a history of the Miners' Federation of Great Britain.* 1949–61, 3 vols.
1498 ——— *A history of the Scottish miners from earliest times.* 1955.
1499 Bagwell, Philip S. *The railwaymen: the history of the National Union of Railwaymen.* 1963. A biased treatment.
1500 Bain, George Sayers. *The growth of white-collar unions.* Oxford, 1970. Especially on the period 1948–64.
1501 Baker, Stanley. *Milk to market: forty years of milk marketing.* 1973. Since the creation of the Milk Marketing Board, 1933.

1502   Barna, Tibor. *Redistribution of incomes through public finance in 1937.*
        Oxford, 1945.
1503   Beckerman, Wilfred. *British economy in 1975.* Cambridge, 1965. Much ref-
        erence to immediate historical background.
1504   —— (ed.). *The Labour government's economic record: 1964—1970.* 1972.
        Various contributors.
1505   Benham, Frederic. *Great Britain under protection.* 1941. Good account of
        depression years.
1506   Best, Robin H. and John T. Coppock. *The changing use of land in Britain.*
        1962. With tables and diagrams; fascinating; and see (1726).
1507   [Birch, Lionel, ed.]. *The history of the T.U.C., 1868—1968.* 1968. Remark-
        able photography with brief, interesting comment.
1508   Bonner, Arnold. *British co-operation: the history, principles and organisation
        of the British co-operative movement.* Manchester, 1961.
1509   Bowley, Arthur L. *Prices and wages in the United Kingdom, 1914—1920.*
        Oxford, 1921.
1510   —— *Some economic consequences of the Great War.* 1930.
1511   —— (ed.). *Studies in national income, 1924—1938.* 1942. A study sponsored
        by the National Institute of Economic and Social Research.
1512   —— *Wages and income in the United Kingdom since 1860.* Cambridge,
        1937. Incorporates earlier studies.
1513   Bowley, Marian. *The British building industry: four studies in response and
        resistance to change.* Cambridge, 1966.
1514   Brandon, Henry. *In the red: the struggle for sterling, 1964—66.* 1966.
1515   Briggs, Asa. *Friends of the people: the centenary history of Lewis's.* 1956.
1516   *Britain in depression: a record of British industries since 1929.* 1935. See also
        Britain in recovery. 1938. Contemporary attitudes; sponsored by the
        British Association for the Advancement of Science.
1517   Broadway, Frank. *State intervention in British industry 1964—68.* Madison,
        N.J., 1969.
1518   Brown, Arthur Joseph. *The great inflation 1939—1951.* 1955. Special concern
        for Britain.
1519   Brown, Kenneth D. *Labour and unemployment 1900—1914.* Totowa, N.J.,
        1971.
1520   Bundock, Clement J. *The national Union of Journalists: a jubilee history,
        1907—1957.* Oxford, 1957.
1521   —— *The story of the National Union of Printing, Bookbinding and Paper
        Workers.* Oxford, 1959.
1522   Burn, Duncan (ed.). *The structure of British industry: a symposium.*
        Cambridge, 1958, 2 vols. Essays on nineteen industries.
1523   Burns, Eveline M. *British unemployment programs, 1920—1938.* Washington,
        D.C., 1941.
1524   Cairncross, Alexander K. (ed.). *The Scottish economy; a statistical account
        of Scottish life.* 1954. Twenty essays, considered 'authoritative', by vari-
        ous writers.
1525   Camps, Miriam. *Britain and the European community, 1955—1963.*
        Princeton, N.J., 1964. Excellent on the 'Common Market'.
1526   Carter, Charles Frederick and Andrew D. Roy. *British economic statistics: a
        report.* Cambridge, 1954. A critical comment on their use.
1527   Cartter, Alan Murray. *The redistribution of income in postwar Britain: a
        study of the effects of the central Government fiscal program in 1948—
        49.* New Haven, Conn., 1955.
1528   Caves, Richard E. *et al. British economic prospects.* 1968. Examines the
        period 1950—65. For its sequel see Cairncross, Alex (ed.), *Britain's econ-
        omic prospects reconsidered.* Albany, N.Y., 1970.
1529   Chapman, Agatha L. and Rose Knight. *Wages and salaries in the United
        Kingdom 1920—1938.* Cambridge, 1953.
1530   Charles, Rodger. *Development of industrial relations in Britain 1911—1939.*
        1973.
1531   Chester, Daniel N. (ed.). *Lessons of the British war economy.* Cambridge,
        1951. Thirteen articles by various authors.

1532   Clark, Colin. *The conditions of economic progress.* 3rd ed., 1955. Presented in a historical context; a significant book.
1533   —— *National income and outlay.* 1937. A revision and extension of his *The national income 1924—1931.* 1932.
1534   Clarke, R.O. *et al. Workers' participation in management in Britain.* 1973. A study carried out at the London School of Economics.
1535   Clegg, Hugh A. *General Union in a changing society — a short history of the National Union of General and Municipal Workers, 1889—1964.* Oxford, 1964.
1536   —— *The system of industrial relations in Great Britain.* 2nd ed., 1972.
1537   Cocks, Edward J. and Bernhardt Walters. *A history of the zinc smelting industry in Britain.* 1968.
1538   Cohen, Percy. *Unemployment insurance and assistance in Britain.* 1938.
1539   Coleman, Donald C. *Courtalds: an economic and social history.* 1969, 2 vols. Vol. II takes the story to 1940.
1540   Crook. W.H. *The general strike: a study of labor's tragic weapon in theory and practice.* Chapel Hill, N.C., 1931. An extensive section on the General Strike of 1926, including interviews with participants.
1541   Croome, David R. and Harry G. Johnson. *Money in Britain 1959—1969.* 1970. Papers to commemorate the tenth anniversary of the report of the Radcliffe Committee on the monetary and credit system, 1957—9.
1542   Davies, Ernest. *National enterprise: the development of the public corporation.* 1946.
1543   Davison, Ronald C. *British unemployment: the modern phase since 1930.* 1938. An earlier study is his *The unemployed: old policies and new.* 1929.
1544   Deakin, Brian M. and T. Seward. *Productivity in transport: a study of employment, capital, output, productivity and technical change.* Cambridge, 1969.
1545   Deane, Phyllis and William A. Cole. *British economic growth, 1688—1959: trends and structure.* 2nd ed., Cambridge, 1967. Significant but severe reading.
1546   Dearle, Norman B. *The Labour cost of the World War to Great Britain 1914—1922.* 1940. 'A statistical analysis'.
1547   Dendy Marshall, Chapman F. *Centenary history of the Liverpool and Manchester Railway.* 1930.
1548   —— *A history of the Southern Railway.* 2nd, enlarged, ed. by R.W. Kidner, 1963, 2 vols.
1549   Devons, Ely. *An introduction to British economic statistics.* Cambridge, 1956. Purpose: 'a general survey of the main British economic statistics'.
1550   Dickie, John P. *The coal problem — a survey: 1910—1936.* 1936.
1551   Dimock, Marshall E. *British public utilities and national development.* 1933. The story after 1918.
1552   Dobb, Maurice Herbert. *Studies in the development of capitalism.* 1947.
1553   Dorfman, Gerald A. *Wage politics in Britain 1945—1967.* Ames, Iowa, 1973. The Government versus the Trades Union Congress.
1554   Dow, John C.R. *The management of the British economy 1945—1960.* Cambridge, 1964.
1555   Dunning, John H. *American investment in British manufacturing industry.* 1958.
1556   Edwards, Ness. *History of the South Wales Miners' Federation.* 1938. Largely from personal knowledge.
1557   Ellis, Hamilton. *British railway history,* vol. II, *1877—1947.* 1959.
1558   —— *Four main lines.* 1950. Ranges over the last century and this.
1559   —— *The Midland Railway.* 2nd ed., 1955.
1560   —— *The South Western Railway, its mechanical history and background 1838—1932.* 1956.
1561   Farman, Christopher. *The General Strike, May 1926.* 1972. Well balanced and well documented; excellent bibliography.
1562   Feinstein, Charles H. *Domestic capital formation in the United Kingdom, 1920—1938.* Cambridge, 1965. The only comprehensive treatment of this period.

1563 —— *National income, expenditure and output of the United Kingdom 1855–1965*. Cambridge, 1972.

1564 Fels, Allan. *The British Prices and Incomes Board*. Cambridge, 1972. A discussion of the role of the Board 1965–70.

1565 Flanagan, Desmond. *1869–1969: a centenary story of the Co-operative Union of Great Britain and Ireland*. Manchester, 1969. Informative but not always reliable.

1566 Flanders, Allan and Hugh A. Clegg. *The system of industrial relations in Great Britain: its history, law and institutions*. 1954.

1567 Fyrth, Hubert J. and Henry Collins. *The foundry workers: a trade union history*. Manchester, 1959.

1568 Garnett, Ronald G. *A century of co-operative insurance*. 1968. The story of the co-operative insurance society, 1867–1967.

1569 Gibbs, C.R. Vernon. *British passenger liners of the five oceans*. 1963. From 1938.

1570 Gilson, Mary Barnett. *Unemployment insurance in Great Britain*. 1931. Concerning the post World War I period to 1930.

1571 Goldstein, Joseph. *The government of a British trade union*. Glencoe, Ill. [1952]. A study of the Transport and General Workers Union.

1572 Goodhart, Charles A.E. *The business of banking 1891–1914*. 1972. Largely statistical.

1573 Grant, Allan John. *Steel and ships: the history of John Brown's*. 1950.

1574 Grant, Alexander T.K. *A study of the capital market in Britain from 1919 to 1936*. 2nd ed., 1967. Reprint, with new introduction of his *A study of the capital market in post-war Britain*. 1937.

1575 Greenleaf, Horace. *Britain's big four: the story of the London Midland and Scottish, London and North Eastern, Great Western, and Southern Railways*. 1948.

1576 Griffin, Alan R. *The miners of Nottinghamshire, 1914–1944: a history of the Nottinghamshire Miners' Union*. 1962.

1577 Gull, Edward M. *British economic interests in the Far East*. 1943. Consideration of the period 1814–1941.

1578 Hall, Alan Ross (ed.). *The export of capital from Britain 1870–1914*. 1968. Essays by various writers.

1579 Hancock, William Keith and Margaret M. Gowing. *British war economy*. 1949. World War II.

1580 Haresnape, Brian. *Railway design since 1830*. 1968–9, 2 vols. Pictorial; vol. II is on 1914–69.

1581 Harris, José. *Unemployment and politics: a study in English social policy 1886–1914*. 1973. Exhaustive and meticulous.

1582 Harris, Nigel. *Competition and the corporate society: British conservatives, the state and industry, 1945–1964*. 1972.

1583 Harrison, Anthony. *The framework of economic activity: the international economy and the rise of the state in the twentieth century*. 1967. Includes detailed discussion of the United Kingdom.

1584 Harrod, Roy F. *The British economy*. New York, 1963.

1585 Hart, Peter E. *Studies in profit, business saving and investment in the United Kingdom, 1920–1962*. 1965–8, 2 vols.

1586 Harte, N.B. (ed.). *The study of economic history*. 1971. Inaugural lectures, including eighteen between 1929 and 1970.

1587 Hawtrey, Ralph G. *Incomes and money*. 1967. 'A criticism of British monetary policy since 1945' in a historical context.

1588 Haynes, William Warren. *Nationalization in practice: the British coal industry*. Boston, 1953. Balanced but with a bias for nationalization.

1589 Henderson, Hubert Douglas. *The inter-war years and other papers*, ed. Henry Clay. Oxford, 1955.

1590 Hibbs, John. *The history of British bus services*. 1968.

1591 Higham, Robin D.S. *Britain's imperial air routes, 1918 to 1939: the story of Britain's overseas airlines*. 1960.

1592 Hill, Arthur C.C. Jr. and Isador Lubin. *The British attack on unemployment*.

1934. A Brookings Institute book; an interesting historical inquiry, showing the atmosphere of the thirties.

1593   Hirst, Francis W. *The consequences of the war to Great Britain*. 1934.

1594   Hodson, Henry V. *Slump and recovery, 1929—1937: a survey of world economic affairs*. 1938. Britain's experience examined in a world context by an authority of the time.

1595   Hunt, E.H. *Regional wage variations in Britain, 1850—1914*. Oxford, 1973.

1596   Hutchinson, Terence W. *Economics and economic policy in Britain, 1946—1966: some aspects of their interrelations*. 1968.

1597   Hutt, Allen. *The condition of the working class in Britain*. 1933. A Marxist view of the thirties and their background. See also his *Post-war history of the British working-class*. 1938.

1598   Hyman, Richard. *The Workers' Union*. Oxford, 1971. On the period 1898—1929.

1599   Ilersic, Alfred R. *Government finance and fiscal policy in post-war Britain*. 1955.

1600   Jacobs, Julius (ed.). *London Trades Council, 1860—1950*. 1950.

1601   Jefferys, James Bovington. *Trade unions in a Labour Britain*. 1947.

1602   Jenkins, Clive. *Power at the top: a critical survey of the nationalized industries*. 1959. On post-1945 developments.

1603   Jevons, H. Stanley. *The British coal trade*. 1915. Excellent on the industry before 1914.

1604   Jones, J. Harry *et al. The coal-mining industry*. 1939. Good survey.

1605   Kahn, Alfred E. *Great Britain in the world economy*. New York, 1946. A study of 1919—39; excellent.

1606   Kelf-Cohen, Reuben. *Twenty years of nationalisation: the British experience*. 1969.

1607   Kenen, Peter B. *British monetary policy and the balance of payments 1951—1957*. Cambridge, Mass., 1960.

1608   Kidd, Howard C. *A new era for British railways*. 1929. Study of Railway Act, 1921.

1609   Kirkaldy, Adam W. (ed.). *British finance during and after the war — 1914—1921*. London, 1921. A contemporary view.

1610   Klapper, Charles F. *The golden age of tramways*. 1961. Detailed.

1611   Knowles, Kenneth G.J.C. *Strikes: a study in industrial conflict with special reference to British experience between 1911 and 1947*. Oxford, 1952. Scholarly.

1612   Lipson, Ephraim. *A planned economy or free enterprise: the lessons of history*. 2nd ed., 1946. A careful inquiry.

1613   Lipton, Michael. *Assessing economic performance*. 1968. 'British economic development 1950—1965 in the light of economic theory and the principles of economic planning'.

1614   Loveday, Arthur. *Britain and world trade*. 1931. Essays on post-war period; Loveday was head of the Economic Intelligence Service of the League of Nations Secretariat.

1615   Lovell, John Christopher and Benjamin C. Roberts. *A short history of the T.U.C.* 1968. Clear, brief, reliable.

1616   Lubin, Isador and Helen Everett. *The British coal dilemma*. 1927.

1617   Lucas, Arthur Fletcher. *Industrial reconstruction and the control of competition: the British experiments*. 1937. Study of British industries between the wars.

1618   Lydall, Harold F. *British incomes and savings*. Oxford, 1955. Based on a survey in 1952.

1619   McCarthy, William E.J. *The closed shop in Britain*. Berkeley, Cal., 1964.

1620   McCloskey, Donald N. *Economic maturity and entrepreneurial decline: British iron and steel, 1870—1913*. Cambridge, Mass., 1973.

1621   MacDermot, Edward Terrence, C.R. Clinker and Oswald S. Nock. *History of the Great Western Railway*. Rev. ed., 1964—7, 3 vols.

1622   MacDonald, Duncan F. *The state and the trade unions*. 1960. Largely on twentieth century.

1623   Mallett, Bernard. *British budgets, 1887–88 to 1912–13, 1913–14 to 1920–21, 1921–22 to 1932–33*. 1913–33, 3 vols. Each budget is analysed.

1624   Martin, Roderick. *Communism and the British trade unions, 1924–1933: a study of the National Minority Movement*. Oxford, 1969.

1625   Marx, Daniel, Jr. *International shipping: a study of industrial self-regulation by shipping conferences*. Princeton, N.J., 1953.

1626   Mess, Henry Adolphis. *Factory legislation and its administration 1891–1924*. 1926. Detailed.

1627   Milne-Bailey, Walter A. *Trade unions and the state*. 1934. In historical context.

1628   Mitchell, Joan. *The National Board for Prices and Incomes*. 1972. An account of the Board, 1965–71.

1629   Moggridge, Donald E. *British monetary policy 1924–1931: the Norman conquest of $4.86*. 1972. See also his *The return to gold in 1925: the formulation of economic policy and its critics*. Cambridge, 1969.

1630   Morgan, E. Victor. *The structure of property ownership in Great Britain*. 1960.

1631   —— *Studies in British financial policy, 1914–25*. 1952.

1632   Morgan, E. Victor and William A. Thomas. *The Stock Exchange: its history and functions*. 2nd ed., 1969.

1633   Morton, Walter A. *British finance 1930–1940*. Madison, Wis., 1943.

1634   Murray, John. *The General Strike of 1926: a history*. 1951. Cf. (1733).

1635   Nicholson, J.L. *Redistribution of income in the United Kingdom in 1959, 1957 and 1953*. 1965. Largely statistical.

1636   Nock, Oswald S. *The Great Western Railway in the twentieth century*. 1964.

1637   Olson, Mancur, Jr. *The economics of the wartime shortage: a history of British food supplies in the Napoleonic War and in World Wars I and II*. Durham, N.C., 1963.

1638   Orton, William Aylott. *Labour in transition: a survey of British industrial history since 1914*. 1921. As it looked then.

1639   Paish, Frank W. *The post war financial problem and other essays*. 1950. Articles originally written in the thirties and forties.

1640   —— *Studies in an inflationary economy: the United Kingdom 1948–1961*. 1962. Articles and papers.

1641   Pearson, Arthur J. *The railways and the nation*. 1964. Immediate background.

1642   Phelps Brown, Ernest H. *The growth of British industrial relations: a study from the standpoint of 1906–14*. 1959. Significant ideas.

1643   —— and Margaret H. Browne. *A century of pay*. New York, 1968. On period 1860–1960.

1644   Pigou, Arthur C. *Aspects of British economic history 1918–1925*. 1947.

1645   Pinder, John H.M. *Britain and the Common Market*. 1961. Brief background.

1646   Prest, Alan R. (ed.). *The U.K. Economy: a manual of applied economics*. 3rd ed., 1970. Collection of articles: much statistical data on the economy since 1950.

1647   —— and A.A. Adams. *Consumers' expenditures in the United Kingdom 1900–1919*. Cambridge, 1954.

1648   Pugh, Arthur. *Men of steel: by one of them: a chronicle of eighty-eight years of trade unionism in the British iron and steel industry*. 1951.

1649   Reader, William J. *Imperial chemical industries: a history*, I, *The forerunners 1870–1926*. 1970.

1650   Reed, Arthur. *Britain's aircraft industry. What went right? What went wrong?* 1973. Journalistic account of developments since 1945.

1651   Reid, Graham L. *et al. The nationalised fuel industries*. 1973.

1652   Richardson, Harry W. *Economic recovery in Britain 1932–9*. 1967. One of the best studies of the economy of the thirties.

1653   —— and Derek H. Aldcroft. *Building in the British economy between the wars*. 1968.

1654   Robbins, Lionel. *The great depression*. 1934.

1655   Roberts, Benjamin C. *National wages policy in war and peace*. 1958. Includes examination of the economy 1939–51.

ECONOMIC HISTORY

1656 —— *The Trades Union Congress 1868–1921*. 1958. Standard.

1657 —— *Trade union government and administration in Great Britain*. 1956.

1658 Robson, Robert. *The cotton industry in Britain*. 1957.

1659 Robson, William A. *Nationalised industry and public ownership*. 1960.

1660 —— (ed.). *Public enterprise: developments in social ownership and control in Great Britain*. 1937. Essays by various writers analysing public boards and commissions.

1661 Rosenberg, Nathan. *Economic planning in the British building industry, 1945–49*. 1960.

1662 Rostas, László. *Comparative productivity in British and American industry*. Cambridge, 1948.

1663 Routh, Guy C. *Occupation and pay in Great Britain, 1906–60*. 1965.

1664 Sanderson, J. Michael. *The universities and British industry 1850–1970*. 1972.

1665 Savage, Christopher I. *An economic history of transport*. 1959. A survey.

1666 Scott, John D. *Vickers: a history*. 1962. Excellent study of armament manufacture.

1667 Seers, Dudley George. *The levelling of incomes since 1938*. Oxford [1951].

1668 Self, Henry and Elizabeth M. Watson. *Electricity supply in Great Britain: its development and organization*. 1952.

1669 Sharp, Ian G. *Industrial conciliation and arbitration in Great Britain*. 1950. Informative.

1670 Sherrington, Charles E.R. *A hundred years of inland transport 1830–1933*. 1934.

1671 Shonfield, Andrew. *Modern capitalism: the changing balance of public and private power*. 1965. Examination of post-war period.

1672 Simmons, Jack. *The railways of Britain: an historical introduction*. 1961. Includes an excellent bibliography.

1673 Simpson, Bill. *Labour, the unions and the party: a study of the trade unions and the British labour movement*. 1973.

1674 Snyder, Rixford Kinney. *The tariff problem in Great Britain, 1918–1923*. Stanford, Cal., 1944.

1675 Spoor, Alec. *White-collar union: sixty years of NALGO*. 1967. A study of the National Association of Local Government Officers, founded in 1905.

1676 Stamp, L. Dudley. *The land of Britain: its use and misuse*. 2nd ed., 1950. A summary and evaluation of the report of the Land Utilisation Survey of Britain, 1930–47.

1677 Stark, Thomas. *The distribution of personal income in the United Kingdom 1949–1963*. Cambridge, 1972.

1678 Stewart, Michael. *Keynes and after*. 1967. A discussion of unemployment and 'full employment' since 1918.

1679 Stone, Richard and D.A. Rowe. *The measurement of consumers' expenditure and behaviour in the United Kingdom 1920–1938*. Cambridge, 1954–66, 2 vols. A massive study.

1680 Strange, Susan. *Sterling and British policy: a political study of an international currency in decline*. 1971. The thesis that the changing status of Sterling was the root cause of economic difficulty in the sixties.

1681 Sturmey, Stanley G. *British shipping and world competition*. 1962. Comprehensive treatment for the twentieth century.

1682 Supple, Barry. *The Royal Exchange Assurance: a history of British insurance 1720–1970*. Cambridge, 1970.

1683 Symons, Julian. *The General Strike: a historical portrait*. 1957. Careful study with accounts by participants.

1684 Tatford, Barrington. *The story of British railways*. [1945.] Informative, popular.

1685 Thomas, Brinley. *Migration and economic growth: a study of Great Britain and the Atlantic economy*. Cambridge, 1954. On the period 1830–1950.

1686 Thomas, David St John and J. Allan Patmore (eds.). *A regional history of the railways of Great Britain*. The series now includes: I, Thomas, David St John, *The west country*. 4th ed., 1973. II, White, H.P., *Southern England*. 3rd ed., 1972. III, White, H.P., *Greater London*, 1963. IV, Hoole, K.,

60

North east England. 1965. V, Gordon, D.I., *The eastern counties.* Newton Abbot, 1968. VI, Thomas, John, *Scotland: The lowlands and the borders.* Newton Abbot, 1971. VII, Christiansen, Rex, *The west midlands.* Newton Abbot, 1973.

1687 Thompson, A.W.J. and L.C. Hunter. *The nationalized transport industries.* 1973. A thorough work of general interest.

1688 Tillyard, Frank and F.N. Ball. *Unemployment insurance in Great Britain, 1911–1948.* 1949. A parliamentary account.

1689 Tomlinson, William Weaver. *Tomlinson's North Eastern Railway: its rise and development,* new ed. with introd. by K. Hoole. Newton Abbot, 1967. Tomlinson's book, originally published in 1915, includes valuable statistics and other information for 1900–14.

1690 Townshend-Rose, H. *The British coal industry.* 1951. On its nationalization.

1691 Turner, Ernest S. *The shocking history of advertising!* New York, 1953.

1692 Turner, Herbert A. *Trade union growth, structure and policy: a comparative study of the cotton unions.* 1962. Sociological approach.

1693 —— *et al. Labour relations in the motor industry: a study of industrial unrest and an international comparison.* 1967.

1694 Vaizey, John. *The brewing industry 1886–1951.* 1960.

1695 —— *The history of British steel.* 1974. For the general reader.

1696 Van der Slice, Austin. *International labor, diplomacy and peace, 1914–1919.* Philadelphia, Pa., 1941. A chapter on the war aims of British labour.

1697 Walker, Gilbert. *Economic planning by programme and control in Great Britain.* 1957.

1698 Webb, Sidney and Beatrice. *The consumers' co-operative movement.* 1921.

1699 Weiner, Herbert E. *British labor and public ownership.* Washington, D.C., 1960. Treated historically throughout the twentieth century.

1700 Wells, Sidney J. *British export performance: a comparative study.* Cambridge, 1964. A study of the fifties.

1701 Wigham, Eric. *The power to manage: a history of the Engineering Employers' Federation.* 1973.

1702 Wilson, Charles H. *The history of Unilever: a study in economic growth and social change.* 1954–68, 3 vols.

1703 Wilson, Geoffrey. *London United Tramways: a history – 1894 to 1933.* 1971.

1704 Worswick, George D.N. and Peter H. Ady (eds.). *The British economy, 1945–1950.* Oxford, 1952. 'Studies of economic development and policies' by various writers; valuable bibliography.

1705 —— *The British economy in the nineteen-fifties.* 1962. Fourteen essays by various authors.

1706 Zupnick, Elliot. *Britain's postwar dollar problem.* New York, 1957.

4 Biographies

1707 Andrews, Philip W.S. and Elizabeth Brunner. *The Life of Lord Nuffield.* 1959.

1708 Bolitho, Hector. *Alfred Mond, First Lord Melchett.* 1933. Best work on Mond.

1709 Boyle, Andrew. *Montagu Norman, a biography.* 1967. See comment by Gregory, Theodore, 'Lord Norman: a new interpretation', *Lloyds Bank Review,* LXXXVIII (Apr. 1968), 31–51.

1710 Clay, Henry. *Lord Norman.* 1957.

1711 Harrod, Roy F. *The life of John Maynard Keynes.* 1951.

1712 Jones, J. Harry. *Josiah Stamp, public servant: the life of the First Baron Stamp of Shortlands.* 1964.

1713 Lawson, Jack. *The man in the cap; the life of Herbert Smith.* 1941. Smith was president of the Miners' Federation, 1921–9.

1714 Pound, Reginald. *Selfridge: a biography.* 1960.

5 Articles

1715 Aldcroft, Derek H. 'The eclipse of English coastal shipping, 1913–21', *JTH,* VI (May 1963), 24–38.

1716 —— 'Railways and economic growth', *JTH*, new ser., I (no. 4, 1973), 238–48.

1717 Alderman, Geoffrey. 'The railway companies and the growth of trade union-ism in the late nineteenth and early twentieth centuries', *Hist. J.*, XIV (no. 1, 1971), 129–52.

1718 Allen, Victor L. 'The reorganization of the Trades Union Congress, 1918–1927', *BJS*, XI (Mar. 1960), 24–43.

1719 Atkin, John. 'Official regulation of British overseas investment, 1914–1931', *EcHR*, XXIII (no. 2, 1970), 324–35.

1720 Bacon, F.W. *et al*, 'The growth of pension rights and their impact on the national economy', *Journal of the Institute of Actuaries*, LXXX (1954), 141–266.

1721 Bagwell, Philip S. 'The Triple Industrial Alliance, 1913–1922', *Ess. Lab. Hist.*, 96–128.

1722 Bain, George Sayers and Robert Price. 'Union growth and employment trends in the United Kingdom 1964–1970', *British Journal of Industrial Relations*, X (Nov. 1972), 366–81.

1723 Baxter, J.L. 'Long-term unemployment in Great Britain, 1953–1971', *Bulletin, Oxford University Institute of Economics and Statistics*, XXXIV (Nov. 1972), 329–44.

1724 Beckerman, Wilfred *et al*, 'The National Plan: a discussion before the Royal Statistical Society ... Nov. 24, 1965', *Journal of the Royal Statistical Society*, ser. A, CXXIX (1966), 1–24. See also (1801).

1725 Bell, R. and E.W. Arkle. 'The London & North Eastern Railway', *JTH*, V (May 1962), 133–45. On the period 1922–48.

1726 Best, Robin H. 'Recent changes and future prospects of land use in England and Wales', *GJ*, CXXXI (Mar. 1965), 1–12. Extends (1506).

1727 Bosanquet, Nicholas and Guy Standing. 'Government and unemployment 1966–1970: a study of policy and evidence'. *British Journal of Industrial Relations*, X (July 1972), 180–92.

1728 Briggs, Asa. 'The world economy: interdependence and planning', in *NCMH*, 37–86.

1729 Brooks, Peter W. 'A short history of London's airports', *JTH*, III (May 1957), 12–22.

1730 Brown, Kenneth D. 'The Trade Union Tariff Association, 1904–1913', *JBS*, IX (May 1970), 141–53.

1731 Chaloner, W.H. 'The British miners and the coal industry between the wars', *History Today*, XIV (June 1964), 418–26.

1732 Chang, Tse Chun. 'The British balance of payments, 1924–1938', *EJ*, LVII (Dec. 1947), 475–503.

1733 Clegg, Hugh A. 'Some consequences of the General Strike', *Transactions of the Manchester Statistical Society*, 1953–4, pp. 1–29.

1734 Cline, Peter K. 'Reopening the case of the Lloyd George coalition and the post war economic transition 1918–1919', *JBS*, X (Nov. 1970), 162–75. Concludes that the coalition government acted in good faith.

1735 Clinton, Alan. 'Trade councils during the First World War., *IRSH*, XV (pt. 2, 1970), 202–34.

1736 Coats, A.W. 'Political economy and the tariff reform campaign of 1903', *Journal of Law and Economics*, XI (Apr. 1968), 181–229.

1737 —— and S.E. Coats. 'The changing social composition of the Royal Economic Society 1890–1960 and the professionalization of British economics', *BJS*, XXIV (June 1973), 165–87.

1738 Court, William H.B. 'Problems of the British coal industry between the wars', *EcHR*, XV (nos. 1–2, 1945), 1–24. Reprinted in his *Scarcity and choice in history*. 1970, pp. 195–224.

1739 —— 'Two economic historians: R.H. Tawney, John H. Clapham', in his *Scarcity and choice in history*. 1970, pp. 127–50.

1740 —— 'The years 1914–1918 in British economic and social history', in his *Scarcity and choice in history*. 1970, pp. 61–126.

1741 Craig, J. *et al*. 'Humberside: employment, unemployment and migration: the evolution of industrial structure 1951—66', *YBESR*, XXII (Nov. 1970), 123—42.

1742 Deane, Phyllis. 'New estimates of gross national product for the United Kingdom, 1830—1914', *Review of Income and Wealth*, XIV (June 1968), 95—112.

1743 Desmarais, Ralph H. 'The British government's strike breaking organization and Black Friday', *JCH*, VI (no. 2, 1971), 112—27.

1744 Fearon, Peter. 'The formative years of the British aircraft industry', *Business History Review*, XLIII (Winter 1969), 476—95.

1745 Galambos, P. and E.W. Evans. 'Work stoppages in the United Kingdom, 1951—64; a quantitative study', *Bulletin, Oxford University Institute of Economics and Statistics*, XXVIII (no. 1, 1966), 33—62. Continued in their 'Work stoppages in the United Kingdom 1965—70; a quantitative study', *Bulletin of Economic Research*, XXV (May 1973), 22—42.

1746 George, Kenneth D. 'The changing structure of competitive industry', *EJ*, LXXXII (Mar. 1972, Supplement), 353—68. On the years 1924—68; technical.

1747 Gilbert, J.C. 'British investment and unit trusts since 1960', *YBESR*, XVII (Nov. 1965), 117—29.

1748 Glenny, M.V. 'The Anglo-Soviet trade agreement, March 1921', *JCH*, V (no. 2, 1970), 63—82.

1749 Gowing, Margaret M. 'The organisation of manpower in Britain during the Second World War', *JCH*, VII (nos. 1—2, 1972), 147—67.

1750 Grant, W.P. and D. Marsh. 'The Confederation of British Industry', *PS*, XIX (1971), 403—15. Its history since formation in July 1965.

1751 Gwilliam, K.M. 'Regulation of air transport', *YBESR*, XVIII (1966), 20—33. Concerned with developments in early sixties.

1752 Hahn, Frank H. and Robert C.O. Matthews. 'The theory of economic growth: a survey', *EJ*, LXXIV (Dec. 1964), 779—902.

1753 Harrison, A.E. 'The competitiveness of the British cycle industry', *EcHR*, 2nd ser., XXII (no. 2, 1969), 287—303.

1754 Hart, Peter E. and Ernest H. Phelps Brown. 'The sizes of trade unions: a study in the laws of aggregation', *EJ*, LXVII (Mar. 1957), 1—15. Examination of the evidence since 1906.

1755 Hartley, Keith. 'The export performance of the British aircraft industry', *Bulletin of Economic Research*, XXIV (Nov. 1972), 81—6.

1756 —— 'The United Kingdom military aircraft market', *YBESR*, XIX (May 1967), 15—36.

1757 Hines, A.G. 'Wage inflation in the United Kingdom 1948—62: a disaggregated study', *EJ*, LXXIX (Mar. 1969), 66—89.

1758 Hinton, James. 'The Clyde Workers' Committee and the dilution struggle', *Ess. Lab. Hist.*, 152—84.

1759 Irving, R.J. 'British railway investment and innovation 1900—1914', *BH*, XIII (Jan. 1971), 39—63.

1760 Jack, Marion. 'The purchase of the British government's shares in the British Petroleum Company 1912—1914', *PP*, XXXIX (April 1968), 139—68.

1761 Jefferys, James B. and Dorothy Walters. 'National income and expenditure of the United Kingdom, 1870—1952', *Income and Wealth*, 5th ser. (1955), 1—40.

1762 Jones, C.D. 'Performance of British Railways, 1962—1968', *Journal of Transport Economics and Policy*, IV (May 1970), 162—70.

1763 Kirby, M.W. 'Government intervention in industrial organization: coal mining in the nineteen thirties', *BH*, XV (July 1973), 160—73.

1764 Knight, K.G. 'Strike and wage inflation in British manufacturing industry, 1950—1968', *Bulletin, Oxford University Institute of Economics and Statistics*, XXXIV (Aug. 1972), 281—94. Technical.

1765 Lauterbach, Albert T. 'Economic demobilization in Great Britain after the First World War', *Political Science Quarterly*, LVII (Sept. 1942), 376—93.

1766 MacDonald, C.A. 'Economic appeasement and the German "moderates" 1937—1939. An introductory essay', *PP*, LVI (Aug. 1972), 105—35.

1767   McDonald, G.W. and Howard F. Gospel. 'The Mond—Turner talks, 1927—
        1933: a study in industrial cooperation', *Hist. J.*, XVI (no. 4, 1973),
        807—29.
1768   Mason, A. 'The Government and the general strike, 1920', *IRSH*, XIV (1969),
        1—21. Uses Cabinet Office papers.
1769   Matthews, Frank. 'The building guilds', *Ess. Lab. Hist.*, 284—331. Guild
        Socialism in the building trades, 1914—26.
1770   Matthews, Robert C.O. 'Some aspects of post-war growth in the British econ-
        omy in relation to historical experience', *Transactions of the Manchester
        Statistical Society* (1964), 3—25. Favourable comment; somewhat
        technical.
1771   —— 'Why has Britain had full employment since the war?', *EJ*, LXXVIII
        (Sept. 1968), 555—69.
1772   Meacham, Standish. ' "The sense of an impending clash": English working-
        class unrest before the First World War', *AHR*, LXXVII (Dec. 1972),
        1343—64.
1773   Mishan, Edward J. 'A survey of welfare economics, 1939—51', *EJ*, LXX (June
        1960), 197—265.
1774   Mogridge, Basil. 'Militancy and inter-union rivalries in British shipping, 1911—
        1929', *IRSH*, VI (1961), 375—412.
1775   Moore, Barry and John Rhodes. 'Evaluating the effects of British regional
        economic policy', *EJ*, LXXXIII (Mar. 1973), 87—110. A study of 1950—
        71.
1776   Nicholson, R.J. 'Capital stock, employment and output in British industry
        1948—64', *YBESR*, XVIII (Nov. 1966), 65—85.
1777   Pencavel, John H. 'An investigation into industrial strike activity in Britain',
        Economica, new ser., XXXVII (Aug. 1970), 239—56. A study of period
        1950—67.
1778   Phelps Brown, Ernest H. and Bernard Weber. 'Accumulation, productivity
        and distribution in the British economy, 1870—1938', *EJ*, LXIII (June
        1953), 263—88.
1779   Phillips, G.A. 'The Triple Industrial Alliance in 1914', *EcHR*, 2nd ser., XXIV
        (no. 1, 1970), 55—67. Discounts possibility of a general strike in 1914.
1780   Pollard, Sidney. 'British and world shipbuilding, 1890—1914: a study in
        comparative costs', *JEcH*, XVII (no. 3, 1957), 426—44.
1781   —— (ed.). *The gold standard and employment policies between the wars*.
        1970. Reprints articles by Edward Nevin, K.J. Hancock, L.J. Hume,
        Sidney Pollard and others.
1782   Porter, J.H. 'Industrial peace in the cotton trade 1875—1913', *YBESR*, XIX
        (May 1967), 49—61.
1783   Quin-Harkin, A.J. 'Imperial airways, 1924—40', *JTH*, I (Nov. 1954), 197—
        215.
1784   Renshaw, Patrick. 'Black Friday, 1921', *History Today*, XXI (June 1971),
        416—25.
1785   Richardson, Harry W. 'The basis of economic recovery in the nineteen-
        thirties: a review and a new interpretation', *EcHR*, 2nd ser., XV (no. 2,
        1962), 344—63.
1786   —— 'The new industries between the wars', *Oxford Economic Papers*, XIII
        (Oct. 1961), 360—84.
1787   Ridley, T.M. 'Industrial production in the United Kingdom 1900—1953',
        Economica, new ser., XXII (Feb. 1955), 1—11.
1788   Robinson, Austin. 'John Maynard Keynes: economist, author, statesman', *EJ*,
        LXXXII (June 1972), 531—46.
1789   Robinson, Olive. 'Representation of the white-collar worker: the Bank Staff
        Associations in Britain', *British Journal of Industrial Relations*, VII (Mar.
        1969), 19—41.
1790   Rowley, J.C.R. 'Fixed capital formation in the British economy, 1956—
        1965', *Economica*, new ser., XXXIX (May 1972), 176—89.
1791   Sanderson, J. Michael. 'The University of London and industrial progress',
        JCH, VII (July—Oct. 1972), 243—62.

1792   Saul, Samuel B. 'The American impact on British industry 1895—1914', *BH*,
       III (Dec. 1960), 19—38.
1793   ——— 'The machine tool industry in Britain to 1914', *BH*, X (Jan. 1968),
       22—43.
1794   ——— 'The motor industry in Britain to 1914', *BH*, V (Dec. 1962), 22—44.
1795   Saville, John (ed.). 'Studies in the British economy 1870—1914', *YBESR*,
       XVII (May 1965 — special issue). Contains Arthur Joseph Brown, 'Britain
       and the world economy, 1870—1914', pp. 46—60; Sidney Pollard, 'Trade
       unions and the labour market 1870—1914', pp. 98—112; W. Ashworth,
       'Changes in industrial structure 1870—1914', pp. 61—74; S.B. Saul, 'The
       export economy, 1870—1914', pp. 5—18.
1796   Sayers, Richard S. 'The springs of technical progress in Britain 1919—39', *EJ*,
       LX (June 1950), 275—91. Already a classic article.
1797   Silver, Michael. 'Recent British strike trends: a factual analysis', *British
       Journal of Industrial Relations*, XI (Mar. 1973), 66—104. Statistical exam-
       ination of the period 1959—71.
1798   Sires, Ronald V. 'Labor unrest in England, 1910—1914', *JEcH*, XV (no. 3,
       1955), 246—66.
1799   Sleeman, John F. 'The British tramway industry: the growth and decline of a
       public utility', *Manchester School of Economic and Social Studies*, X
       (1939), 157—74.
1800   Stolper, Wolfgang Frederick. 'British monetary policy and the housing boom',
       Quarterly Journal of Economics, LVI (Nov. 1941), pt. 2.
1801   Surrey, M.J.C. 'The National Plan in retrospect', *Bulletin of the Oxford Insti-
       tute of Economics and Statistics*, XXXIV (Aug. 1972), 249—68. See also
       (1724).
1802   Tawney, Richard H. 'The abolition of economic controls, 1918—1921',
       EcHR, XIII (1943), 1—30.
1803   Turner, Herbert A. 'The Donovan Report', *EJ*, LXXIX (Mar. 1969), 1—10.
       See (1456).
1804   Usher, Abbot Payson. 'Sir John Howard Clapham and the empirical reaction
       in economic history', *JEcH*, XI (no. 2, 1951), 148—53. A critique of
       Clapham's *The study of economic history* (Cambridge, 1929).
1805   Veverka, J. 'The growth of government expenditure in the United Kingdom
       since 1790', *Scottish Journal of Political Economy*, X (Feb. 1963), 111—
       27.
1806   Wadsworth, John E. (ed.). *The banks and the monetary system in the U.K.,
       1959—1971*. 1973. Reprint of articles in *Midland Bank Review*.
1807   Williams, David. 'London and the 1931 financial crisis', *EcHR*, 2nd ser., XV
       (no. 3, 1963), 513—28.
1808   Williams, J.E. 'The political activities of a trade union, 1906—1914', *IRSH*,
       II (pt. 1, 1957), 1—21. In Derbyshire.
1809   Woodruffe, Kathleen. 'The making of the welfare state in England: a sum-
       mary of its origin and development', *Journal of Social History*, I (no. 4,
       1968), 303—24.
1810   Zebel, Sydney H. 'Joseph Chamberlain and the genesis of tariff reform', *JBS*,
       VII (Nov. 1967), 131—57. Informative.

IX. URBAN HISTORY
(See introductory remarks in Preface.)

1 Printed sources

1811   Abercrombie, Patrick. *Greater London plan, 1944*. 1945. A master plan for
       'renewal and dispersal'; complements the County of London plan (1813).
1812   Booth, Charles. *Life and labour of the people in London*. 1902—3, 17 vols.
       A study of poverty, industry, religious and social influences. See (1814)
       for a later survey.

1813   Forshaw, John H. and Patrick Abercrombie. *County of London plan prepared for the London County Council.* 1944. Like (1811), a celebrated war time report.

1814   *New Survey of London life and labour.* 1930—35, 9 vols. Prepared by the London School of Economics and Political Science; various authors. Cf. (1812).

1815   Roberts, Robert. *The classic slum: Salford life in the first quarter of the century.* Manchester, 1971. A combination of 'personal reminiscence' and 'research'.

1816   Rowntree, B. Seebohm. *Poverty: a study in town life.* 1901. A classic study of York, based upon a house-to-house canvass. See also his *Poverty and progress.* 1941. This was based on a survey of York made in 1936. And see (1817).

1817   —— and George R. Lavers. *Poverty and the welfare state: a third social survey of York dealing only with economic questions.* 1951.

2 Surveys

1818   Abercrombie, Patrick. *Town and country planning.* 3rd ed., rev. by D. Rigby Childs. 1959. A very useful survey.

1819   Finer, Herman. *English local government.* 4th ed., 1950. Standard.

1820   Griffith, Ernest S. *The modern development of city government in the United Kingdom and the United States.* 1927, 2 vols.

3 Monographs

1821   Barker, Brian. *Labour in London: a study in municipal achievement.* 1946.

1822   Bealey, Frank and J. Blondell and W.P. McCann. *Constituency politics: a study of Newcastle-under-Lyme.* 1965.

1823   Buchanan Report. *Traffic in towns: a study of the long term problems of traffic in urban areas. Reports of the steering group and working group appointed by the minister of transport.* 1963.

1824   Burns, Wilfred. *New town for old: the technique of urban renewal.* 1963. Post 1945 developments.

1825   Chapman, Stanley D. (ed.). *The history of working class housing: a symposium.* Newton Abbot, 1971. Case studies from several urban industrial areas.

1826   Coppock, John T. and Hugh C. Prince (eds.). *Greater London.* 1964. Essays.

1827   Creese, Walter L. *The search for environment. The garden city: before and after.* 1906.

1828   Cullingworth, John B. *Town and country planning in England and Wales, an introduction.* 1964.

1829   Donnison, David V. *et al. Social policy and administration: studies in the development of social services at the local level.* 1965.

1830   Evans, Hazel (ed.). *New towns: the British experience.* 1973.

1831   Foley, Donald L. *Controlling London's growth: planning the Great Wen 1940—1960.* Berkeley, Cal., 1963. Continued by his *Governing the London region: reorganization and planning in the 1960's.* Berkeley, Cal., 1972.

1832   Freeman, T.W. *The conurbations of Great Britain.* 2nd ed., Manchester, 1966.

1833   —— *Geography and regional administration, England and Wales 1830—1968.* 1968. Attention 'to local government units as areas'.

1834   Garside, William R. *The Durham miners, 1919—1960.* 1971. Thorough.

1835   Gibbon, Gwilym and Reginald W. Bell. *History of the London County Council, 1899—1939.* 1939.

1836   Gill, Conrad and Asa Briggs. *History of Birmingham, II, Borough and City 1865—1938.* 1952. For vol. III, see (1859).

1837   Griffith, John A.G. *Central departments and local authorities.* 1966. Contemporary problems with historical background.

1838   Hall, Peter *et al. The containment of urban England.* 1973, 2 vols. A judgment on town planning since 1940.

1839 Harris, John S. *British government inspection: the local services and the central departments*. 1955.
1840 Hawson, H. Keeble. *Sheffield: the growth of a city, 1893—1926*. Sheffield, 1968.
1841 Hyde, Francis E. *Liverpool and the Mersey: an economic history of a port 1700—1970*. 1971.
1842 Jones, D. Caradog (ed.). *The social survey of Merseyside*. Liverpool, 1934. Based on a survey, 1929—32.
1843 Lipman, Vivian D. *Local government areas 1834—1945*. Oxford, 1949.
1844 Lovell, John. *Stevedores and dockers: a study of trade unionism in the Port of London, 1870—1914*. 1969.
1845 MacInnes, Charles M. *Bristol at war*. London, 1962. On World War II.
1846 Maclure, Stuart. *One hundred years of London education, 1870—1970*. 1970.
1847 Martin, John E. *Greater London: an industrial geography*. 1966. Much attention to the past.
1848 Mellish, Michael. *The docks after Devlin: a study of the effects of the recommendations of the Devlin Committee on industrial relations in the London docks*. 1973. Studies pursued at the London School of Economics.
1849 Osborn, Frederic J. and Arnold Whittick. *The new towns: the answer to Megalopolis*. Rev. ed., 1969. Developments since 1939.
1850 Pimlott, John A.R. *Toynbee Hall: fifty years of social progress, 1884—1934*. 1935.
1851 Pollard, Sidney. *A history of labour in Sheffield*. Liverpool, 1959. A pioneer work.
1852 Rhodes, Gerald. *The government of London: the struggle for reform*. 1970. Contemporary problems in historical context.
1853 Richardson, Kenneth and Elizabeth Harris. *Twentieth-century Coventry*. 1972.
1854 Robson, William A. *Government and misgovernment of London*. 1939.
1855 Rodgers, Barbara N. and June Stevenson. *A new portrait of social work; a study of the social services in a northern town from Younghusband to Seebohm*. 1973. See also Barbara N. Rodgers and Julia Dixon, *Portrait of social work: a study of social services in a northern town*. Oxford, 1960.
1856 Sansom, William. *Westminster at war*. 1947. One of the best accounts of the *Blitz* in London.
1857 Scott, Mackay H. Baillie *et al. Garden suburbs, town planning and modern architecture*. 1910.
1858 Simmons, Jack. *Leicester past and present*, II, Modern City, 1860—1974. 1974.
1859 Sutcliffe, Anthony and Roger Smith. *History of Birmingham*, III, Birmingham 1939—1970. Oxford, 1974. For vol. II, see (1836).
1860 Thompson, Francis M.L. *Hampstead: building a borough 1650—1964*. 1974. An 'emphasis . . . on the process of the creation of the urban environment'.

4 Biographies

1861 Stocks, Mary. *Ernest Simon of Manchester*. Manchester, 1963. Biography of an industrialist and public servant.

5 Articles

1862 Bealey, Frank and David J. Bartholomew. 'The local election in Newcastle-under-Lyme, May 1958', *BJS*, XIII (Sept., Dec., 1962), 273—85, 350—68. Based on a survey of opinion and voting intention five days before the election.
1863 Benjamin, Bernard. 'The urban background to public health changes in England and Wales, 1900—1950', *Population Studies*, XVII (1963—4), 225—48.
1864 Bowley, Marian E.A. 'Local authorities and housing subsidies since 1919', *Manchester School of Economic and Social Studies*, XII (1941), 57—79.

1865   Cherry, Gordon E. 'Influences on the development of town planning in Britain', *JCH*, V (July 1969), 43–58.
1866   Clarke, Peter F. 'British politics and Blackburn politics, 1900–1910', *Hist. J.*, XII (no. 2, 1969), 302–27.
1867   Connor, L.R. 'Urban housing in England and Wales', *Journal, Royal Statistical Society*, LXIX (1936), 1–66. 'A discussion of housing reform from a statistical point of view.'
1868   George, Wilma. 'Social conditions and the Labour vote in the county boroughs of England and Wales', *BJS*, II (no. 3, 1951), 255–9.
1869   Gibbon, I.G. 'Recent changes in the local government of England and Wales', *American Political Science Review*, XXIII (Aug. 1929), 633–56. Historical background of the Local Government Act of 1929.
1870   Jenkins, Simon. 'Decline and fall of London town', *Encounter*, XXXV (Oct. 1970), 77–84. Changes during World War II and after.
1871   Murphy, Lawrence R. 'Rebuilding Britain: the Government's role in housing and town planning, 1945–57', *Historian*, XXXII (May 1970), 410–27.
1872   Stedman, M.B. and P.A. Wood. 'Urban renewal in Birmingham: an interim report', *Geography*, L (1965), 1–17. Developments since 1945.
1873   Thomas, Brinley. 'The influx of labour into the midlands, 1920–37', *Economica*, new ser., V (Nov. 1938), 410–34.
1874   —— The movement of labour into south-east England, 1920–32. *Economica*, new ser., I (May 1934), 220–41.
1875   Walker, Gilbert. 'The growth of population in Birmingham and the Black Country between the wars', *University of Birmingham Historical Journal*, I (1947–8), 158–79.
1876   Williams, J.E. 'The Leeds Corporation strike in 1913', *Ess. Lab. Hist.*, 70–95.
1877   Wilson, Norman. 'The local government service since the war', *PA*, XXX (Spring 1952), 131–8.
1878   Wise, M.J. 'The Birmingham Black Country in its regional setting', *Geography*, LVII (Apr. 1972), 89–104.
1879   Wright, H. Myles. 'The first ten years: post-war planning and development in England', *Town Planning Review*, XXVI (July 1955), 73–92.

X. AGRICULTURAL HISTORY

1 Printed sources

1880   Bensusan, Samuel L. *Latter-day rural England 1927*. 1928. Based on four months visit to agricultural counties.
1881   Ernle, Rowland Edmund Prothero, Lord. *Whippingham to Westminster*. 1938. Reminiscences of a leading agriculturalist.
1882   Ministry of Agriculture, Fisheries and Food. *A century of agricultural statistics, Great Britain, 1866–1966*. 1968.
1883   Pratt, Edwin A. *The transition in agriculture*. 1906. As it looked early in the century.
1884   Thompson, Flora. *Lark Rise to Candleford: a trilogy*. 1945. On rural society.

2 Surveys

1885   Ernle, Rowland Edmund Prothero, Lord. *English farming, past and present. With introductions by George E. Fussell and Oliver R. McGregor*. 6th ed., 1961.
1886   Green, Frederick E.A. *A history of the English agricultural labourer, 1870–1920*. 1920.
1887   Harvey, Nigel. *The farming kingdom*. 1955. On transformation in twentieth century.
1888   Russell, E. John. *A history of agricultural science in Great Britain 1620–1954*. 1966. More than half is devoted to the twentieth century.
1889   Symon, J.A. *Scottish farming past and present*. Edinburgh, 1959.

1890   Trow-Smith, Robert. *English husbandry, from the earliest times to the present day.* 1951.

3 Monographs

1891   *Agriculture in the twentieth century.* Oxford, 1939. Essays by various specialists to be presented to Sir Daniel Hall.

1892   Astor, Waldorf, 2nd Viscount and B. Seebohm Rowntree. *British agriculture: the principles of future policy.* 1939. Useful for the inter-war years.

1893   Bateson, Frederick W. (ed.). *Towards a socialist agriculture: studies by a group of Fabians.* 1946.

1894   Groves, Reg. *Sharpen the sickle! The history of the Farm Workers' Union.* 1949.

1895   Hall, Alfred Daniel. *Agriculture after the war.* 1916. A plan for reorganization developed more fully in his *Reconstruction and the land.* 1941.

1896   Hurd, Archibald R. *A farmer in Whitehall: Britain's farming revolution, 1939—1950.* 1951.

1897   Jones, Eric L. *Seasons and prices: the role of the weather in English agricultural history.* 1964.

1898   Layton, Walter T. and Geoffrey Crowther. *An introduction to the study of prices.* 1935.

1899   Levy, Hermann. *Large and small holdings: a study of English agricultural economics.* 1911.

1900   Mejer, Eugeniusz. *Agricultural labour in England and Wales.* Sutton Bonington, 1949—51, 2 parts.

1901   Murray, Keith A.H. *Agriculture.* 1955. During World War II, with useful introduction for 1914—39.

1902   Ojala, Eric M. *Agriculture and economic progress.* 1952. Comparative study of the U.K., Sweden and U.S.A., based on a statistical inquiry.

1903   Orwin, Charles S. and William R. Peel. *The tenure of agricultural land.* 2nd ed., Cambridge, 1926.

1904   Perry, P.J. (ed.). *British agriculture 1875—1914.* 1973. Essays reinterpreting 'the agricultural crisis'.

1905   ——— *British farming in the great depression 1870—1914: an historical geography.* Newton Abbot, 1974. Excellent bibliography.

1906   Robertson Scott, J.W. *The story of the Women's Institute movement in England and Wales and Scotland.* Idbury, Kingham, Oxon., 1925.

1907   Savage, William G. *Rural housing.* 1915.

1908   Saville, John. *Rural depopulation in England and Wales 1851—1951.* 1957.

1909   Self, Peter and Herbert J. Storing. *The state and the farmer.* 1962. On the post-1945 period.

1910   Sutherland, Douglas. *The landowners.* 1968.

1911   Whetham, Edith H. *British farming, 1939—49.* 1952.

1912   Williams, H.T. (ed.). *Principles for British agricultural policy.* 1960. Report of a committee of experts representing agricultural science, sociology, economics and human nutrition; includes useful historical section.

4 Biographies

1913   Ashby, Mabel K. *Joseph Ashby of Tysoe, 1859—1919: a study of English village life.* Cambridge, 1961. In Warwickshire.

1914   Dale, Harold E. *Daniel Hall, pioneer in scientific agriculture.* 1956.

5 Articles

1915   Chew, Hilary C. 'Changes in land use and stock over England and Wales, 1939 to 1951', *GJ*, CXXII (Dec. 1956), 466—70.

1916   Coppock, John T. 'The changing arable in England and Wales 1870—1956', *Tijdschrift voor Economische en sociale Geografie*, L (no. 6—7, 1959), 121—30.

1917   Ernle, Rowland Edmund Prothero, Lord. 'The food campaign of 1916—18',

Journal of the Royal Agricultural Society of England, LXXXII (1922), 1–48.

1918 Hallett, Graham. 'The economic position of British agriculture', *EJ*, LXIX (Sept. 1959), 522–40. On the early fifties.

1919 Kirk, J.H. 'The output of British agriculture during the war', *Journal of the Proceedings of the Agricultural Economics Society*, VII (June 1946), 30–45.

1920 Orton, C.R. 'The development of stratified sampling methods for the agricultural census of England and Wales', *Journal of the Royal Statistical Society*, ser A, CXXXV (1972), 307–35.

1921 Orwin, Charles S. 'Commodity prices and farming policy', *Journal of the Royal Agricultural Society of England*, LXXXIII (1922), 3–14. On fortunes of agriculture in early twentieth century.

1922 Perren, R. 'The North American beef and cattle trade with Great Britain, 1870–1914', *EcHR*, ser. 2, XXIV (no. 3, 1971), 430–44.

1923 Voelcker, J. Augustus. 'Woburn and its work 1876–1921', *Journal of the Royal Agricultural Society of England*, LXXXIV (1923), 110–66.

1924 Whetham, Edith H. 'The mechanisation of British farming 1910–1945', *Journal of Agricultural Economics*, XXXI (Sept. 1960), 317–31.

1925 —— et al. *A record of agricultural policy, 1947–1952, 1952–1954, 1954–1956, 1956–1958, 1958–1960*. Cambridge, 1952–. Occasional Papers, Cambridge University School of Agriculture.

XI. SCIENCE AND TECHNOLOGY

1 Printed sources

1926 Badash, Lawrence (ed.). *Rutherford and Boltwood: letters on radioactivity*. 1969. During the years 1904–24.

1927 Brabazon, John Theodore Cuthbert Moore, 1st Baron. *The Brabazon story*. 1966.

1928 Brock, William H. (ed.). *H.E. Armstrong and the teaching of science 1880–1930*. Cambridge, 1973. Essays.

1929 Crowther, James Gerald. *The social relations of science*. New York, 1941.

1930 Eddington, Arthur S. *The mathematical theory of relativity*. 2nd ed., 1924.

1931 —— *The nature of the physical world*. 1928.

1932 Haldane, J.S. *The sciences and philosophy*. 1929. Gifford Lectures, Glasgow, 1927–28.

1933 Holliday, Leslie (ed.). *The integration of technologies*. 1966. A group of essays 'searching for the common ground between different technologies'.

1934 Hutton, Robert S. *Recollections of a technologist*. 1964. By an authority in metallurgy.

1935 Huxley, Julian. *Memories I; Memories II*. 1970, 1973. Autobiography of a celebrated biologist.

1936 Jeans, James Hopwood. *Astronomy and cosmogony*. 1928. Attempts to describe the present position of cosmogony and . . . associated problems of astronomy.

1937 —— *The universe around us*. 1929. 'A brief account, written in simple language, of the methods and results of modern astronomical research' (Preface).

1938 Russell, Bertrand. *The A B C of atoms*. 1923.

1939 —— *Our knowledge of the external world as a field for scientific method in philosophy*. 1914.

1940 Whitehead, Alfred North. *Science and the modern world*. 1926.

1941 Zuckerman, Solly. *Scientists and war: the impact of science on military and civil affairs*. 1966.

2 Surveys

1942   Cardwell, Donald S.L. *Organisation of science in England: a retrospect*. 2nd ed., Melbourne, 1957. A history of scientific education.

1943   —— *Turning points in western technology: a study of technology, science and history*. New York, 1972.

1944   Crombie, Alistair C. (ed.). *Scientific change: historical studies in the intellectual, social and technical conditions for scientific discovery and technical invention, from antiquity to the present*. 1963. A symposium on the history of science at Oxford, 9—15 July 1961.

1945   Crowther, James Gerald. *Discoveries and inventions of the 20th century*. 5th ed., 1966.

1946   Dampier [-Whetham], William Cecil. *A history of science and its relations with philosophy and religion*. 4th ed., Cambridge, 1948. Reprinted with a postscript by I. Bernard Cohen. Cambridge, 1966.

1947   Dingle, Herbert (ed.). *A century of science, 1851—1951*. 1951.

1948   Dunsheath, Percy (ed.). *A century of technology 1851—1951*, New York, [1951]. By 'specialist authors' in various fields of industry.

1949   Fyrth, Hubert J. and Maurice Goldsmith. *Science, history and technology*. Book 2, pt. 2, *The age of uncertainty, the 1880s to the 1940s*. Book 2, pt. 3, *The age of choice: the 1940s to the 1960s*. 1969.

1950   Harré, H. Romano (ed.). *Scientific thought 1900—1960: a selective survey*. 1969. Essays on twelve areas.

1951   Mason, Stephen F. *Main currents of scientific thought: a history of the sciences*. New York, 1953.

1952   Singer, Charles and E. Ashworth Underwood. *A short history of medicine*. 2nd ed., 1962. A good reference work.

3 Monographs

1953   Ahrons, Ernest L. *The British steam railway locomotive 1825—1925*. 1927. Continued in Nock, Oswald S. *The British steam railway locomotive, 1925—65*. 1966.

1954   Allibone, T.E. *Rutherford, the father of nuclear energy*. Manchester, 1973. The Rutherford lecture at Manchester U., 1972.

1955   Baker, W.J. *A history of the Marconi Company*. 1970.

1956   Birks, John B. (ed.). *Rutherford at Manchester*. 1962. Commemorative essays together with correspondence and scientific papers of the noted physicist.

1957   Clair, Colin. *A history of printing in Britain*. 1965.

1958   Clark, Ronald W. *The birth of the bomb: the untold story of Britain's part in the weapon that changed the world*. 1961. See also Gowing, Margaret M. *Britain and atomic energy, 1939—1945*. 1964.

1959   Crowther, James Gerald and R. Whiddington. *Science at war*. 1947. Excellent for the lay reader.

1960   Dronamraju, K.R. (ed.). *Haldane and modern biology*. Baltimore, Md., 1968.

1961   Dunsheath, Percy A. *A history of electrical engineering*. 1962.

1962   Fletcher, Harold R. *The story of the Royal Horticultural Society, 1804—1968*. 1969.

1963   Freeman, T.W. *One hundred years of geography*. 1961. 'Written with a basis of British geography.'

1964   Gale, Walter K.V. *The British iron and steel industry: a technical history*. Newton Abbot, 1967.

1965   Gibbs-Smith, Charles H. *The aeroplane: an historical survey of its origins and development*. 1960. Excellent on Britain's role.

1966   Hall, A. Rupert. *The Cambridge Philosophical Society: a history, 1819—1969*. Cambridge, 1969.

1967   Hardie, David W.F. and J. Davidson Pratt. *A history of the modern British chemical industry*. 1966. Of general interest.

1968   Hearnshaw, Leslie S. *A short history of British psychology 1840—1940*. New York, 1964.

1969   Hilken, Thomas J.N. *Engineering at Cambridge University, 1783–1965*. 1967.

1970   Hunt, Thomas (ed.). *The Medical Society of London 1773–1973*. 1972.

1971   Kidner, R.W. *A short history of mechanical traction and travel*. 1946–7, 6 parts. Parts 5 and 6 concern locomotives and carriages in twentieth century.

1972   Lock, Robert Heath. *Recent progress in the study of variation, heredity and evolution*. 4th ed., 1916.

1973   Nayler, Joseph and Ernest Ower. *Aviation: its technical development*. 1965.

1974   Newsholme, Arthur. *The story of modern preventive medicine*. 1929.

1975   Nock, Oswald S. *Steam locomotives: the unfinished story of steam locomotives and steam locomotive men on the railways of Great Britain*. 1957.

1976   —— *The locomotives of Sir Nigel Gresley*. 1945. Concerning 'the most notable English locomotive engineer' of his time. See also Nock's *The locomotives of R.E.L. Maunsell, 1911–1937*. Bristol. 1954.

1977   North, John D. *The measure of the universe. A history of modern cosmology*. 1965.

1978   Payne, George Louis. *Britain's scientific and technological manpower*. 1960. Important chapters on expansion of technological education and research after World War II.

1979   Penrose, Harald. *British aviation: the pioneer years 1903–1914*. 1967. Continued by his *British aviation; the Great War and armistice 1915–1919*. New York, 1969. Also, *British aviation: the adventuring years 1920–1929*. 1973.

1980   *Perkin centenary: 100 years of synthetic dyestuffs*. 1958. Includes the 'life and work of Professor W.H. Perkin' (1838–1907) and developments thereafter.

1981   Rolt, Lionel T.C. *Tools for the job: a short history of machine tools*. 1965.

1982   Rowe, A.P. *One story of radar*. Cambridge, 1948. Concerns the governmental department, The Telecommunications Research Establishment, from 1934 to 1945.

1983   Rutherford, Ernest, Baron. *The newer alchemy*. Cambridge, 1937. 'A brief account of modern work on the transmutation of the elements.'

1984   Shorter, Alfred H. *Paper making in the British Isles: a historical and geographical study*. Newton Abbot, 1971. A standard work.

1985   Snow, Charles Percy, Baron. *Science and government*. Cambridge, 1961. Lectures on Henry Tizard, F.A. Lindemann and World War II.

1986   Swazey, Judith P. *Reflexes and motor integration: Sherrington's concept of integrative action*. Cambridge, Mass., 1969. Sherrington (1859–1932) was a leader in neuro-physiology.

1987   Vaughan, Paul. *Doctors' Commons, a short history of the British Medical Association*. 1959.

1988   Webb, Brian. *The British internal combustion locomotive 1894–1940*. Newton Abbot, 1973.

1989   Whittaker, Edmund. *A history of the theories of aether and electricity*, II, *The modern theories 1900–1926*. 1953.

1990   Wilson, William. *A hundred years of physics*. 1950.

4 Biographies

1991   Armytage, Walter H.G. *Sir Richard Gregory: his life and work*. 1957. Gregory was a scientific journalist, editor of *Nature*, 1919–39.

1992   Bickel, Lennard. *Rise up to life: a biography of Howard Walter Florey who gave penicillin to the world*. 1972.

1993   Clark, Ronald. *Sir Edward Appleton*. 1971. Biography of a noted physicist.

1994   —— *J.B.S.: the life and work of J.B.S. Haldane*. 1968.

1995   —— *Tizard*. 1965. Concerning Sir Henry Tizard and radar.

1996   Crowther, James Gerald. *British scientists of the twentieth century*. 1952. Essays on J.J. Thomson, Ernest Rutherford, J.H. Jeans, A.S. Eddington, F.G. Hopkins and William Bateson.

1997   —— *Statesmen of science*. 1965. Includes R.B. Haldane, H.T. Tizard, and F.A. Lindemann. 1965.

1998 Eve, A.S. *Rutherford: being the life and letters of the Rt. Hon. Lord Rutherford, O.M.* Cambridge, 1939.
1999 Granit, Ragnar. *Charles Scott Sherrington: an appraisal.* 1966.
2000 Gunther, Albert E. *Robert T. Gunther: a pioneer in the history of science 1869–1940.* 1967.
2001 Harrod, Roy F. *The Prof: a personal memoir of Lord Cherwell.* 1959.
2002 Heilbron, John L. *H.G.J. Moseley: the life and letters of an English physicist, 1887–1915.* 1973.
2003 Kilmister, Clive W. *Men of physics: Sir Arthur Eddington.* Oxford, 1966.
2004 Lockyer, T. Mary and Winifred L. *Life and work of Sir Norman Lockyer.* 1928.
2005 Pogson, Beryl. *Maurice Nicoll: a portrait.* 1961. Of a well-known psychiatrist.
2006 Thomson, George P. *J.J. Thomson and the Cavendish Laboratory in his day.* 1964. Published in the United States as *J.J. Thomson, discoverer of the electron.* New York, 1966. For Thomson's association with the Cavendish Laboratory, see Crowther, James Gerald, *The Cavendish Laboratory 1874–1974.* 1974.

5 Articles

2007 Crone, G.R. 'British geography in the twentieth century', *GJ*, CXXX (June 1964), 197–220.
2008 De Beer, Gavin. 'Mendel, Darwin, and Fisher (1865–1965)', *Notes and Records of the Royal Society of London*, XIX (Dec. 1964), 192–226.
2009 Fleure, H.J. 'Sixty years of geography and education: a retrospect of the Geographical Association', *Geography*, XXXVIII (Nov. 1953), 231–65. On the period 1890–1950.
2010 Goldberg, Stanley. 'In defense of ether: the British response to Einstein's special theory of relativity, 1905–1911', in Russell McCormmach (ed.), *Historical studies in the physical sciences*, II, Philadelphia, 1970.
2011 McCormmach, Russell. 'J.J. Thomson and the structure of light', *British Journal for the History of Science*, III (1966–67), 362–87.
2012 McKie, Douglas, 'Science and technology', in *NCMH*, 87–111.
2013 *The Newcomen Society for the Study of the History of Engineering and Technology: transactions.* Vol. I (1920–1)–. Some 40 volumes have been published, covering the story to 1968. Valuable for information on 'the lives and works of men who have laid the foundations of our present industries'.
2014 Venables. P.F.R. 'The emergence of colleges of advanced technology in Britain', *The Year Book of Education 1959*. New York, 1959, pp. 224–36. On developments after 1944.

XII. MILITARY AND NAVAL HISTORY

(For guidance to the literature of this topic the advanced student is at once referred to (26). Indispensable for the two world wars are the 'Official Histories', published by H.M.S.O., on which see (27); the major categories with key items are listed in (2050) and (2051)).

1 Printed sources

2015 Bell, Julian (ed.). *We did not fight: 1914–1918 experiences of war resisters.* 1935.
2016 Blake, Robert (ed.). *The private papers of Douglas Haig 1914–1919.* 1952. A selection. See also (2067).
2017 Churchill, Winston Spencer. *The Second World War.* Boston, Mass., 1948–53, 6 vols.
2018 Flower, Desmond and James Reeves (eds.). *The war, 1939–1945.* 1960. Documentary.

2019 Fremantle, Sydney R. *My naval career 1880—1928*. 1949. One of the more useful naval memoirs.

2020 Graves, Robert. *Goodbye to all that*. New York, 1930. One of the finest auto-biographical books on World War I. Another, on 1916—17, is Sassoon, Siegfried, *Memoirs of an infantry officer*. New York, 1930.

2021 Ismay, Hastings Lionel, 1st Baron. *The memoirs of General Lord Ismay*. 1960. Ismay was deputy secretary (military) to the War Cabinet, 1940—5, and chief of staff to the minister of defense (Churchill), 1940—5.

2022 Jellicoe, John Rushworth, 1st Earl. *The Grand Fleet, 1914—1916*. New York, 1919. See also Patterson, A. Temple (ed.). *The Jellicoe papers: selections from the private and official correspondence of Admiral of the Fleet Earl Jellicoe of Scapa*. 1966—8, 2 vols. Patterson's biography, *Jellicoe* (1969) is standard.

2023 Keyes, Roger. *The naval memoirs of Admiral of the Fleet Sir Roger Keyes*: [I] *The Narrow Seas to the Dardanelles, 1910—1915*; [II] *Scapa Flow to the Dover Straits, 1916—1918*. 1934—5, 2 vols.

2024 MacLeod, Roderick and Denis Kelley (eds.). *The Ironside Diaries 1937—1940*. 1962. In the United States published as *Time unguarded*. Valuable for events of 1939. See also Ironside, Edmund Oslac, 2nd Baron (ed.), *High road to command: the diaries of Major General Sir Edmund Ironside, 1920—1922*. 1972.

2025 Montague, Charles E. *Disenchantment*. New York, 1922. A classic account of conditions at the front in World War I. for another sensitive account see Carrington, Charles E. *Soldier from the wars returning*. 1964.

2026 Montgomery, Bernard Law, 1st Viscount. *The memoirs of Field-Marshal the Viscount Montgomery of Alamein, K.G.* Cleveland, Ohio, 1958. See also Moorehead, Alan, *Montgomery, a biography* (New York, 1946).

2027 Pownall, Henry. *Chief of staff: the diaries of Lieutenant-General Sir Henry Pownall*, I, *1933—1940*, ed. Brian Bond. 1973.

2028 Robertson, William Robert. *Soldiers and statesmen, 1914—1918*. 1926. See also his *From private to field-marshal*. 1921. The first volume is vital for an analysis of strategy. And see Bonham-Carter, Victor, *Soldier true: the life and times of Field-Marshal Sir William Robertson . . . 1860—1933*. 1963.

2029 Slim, William. *Defeat into victory*. 1956. Probably the best account of the Burma campaign, written by the general in command. On treatment of Wingate, cf. Sykes, Christopher, *Orde Wingate*. 1959.

2030 Tedder, Arthur, Lord. *With prejudice*. This account rings true, as does Harris, Arthur, *Bomber offensive*. New York, 1947.

2031 Wilson, Henry Maitland, Baron. *Eight years overseas, 1939—1947*. By the supreme allied commander, Mediterranean, 1943—4.

2 Surveys

2032 Barnett, Correlli. *Britain and her army, 1509—1970: a military, political and social survey*. 1970.

2033 Kemp, Peter (ed.). *History of the Royal Navy*. 1969. Kemp is also the author of *Victory at sea 1939—1945*. 1957.

2034 Schofield, B.B. *British sea power: naval policy in the twentieth century*. 1967.

3 Monographs

2035 Barker, Arthur J. *Suez: the seven day war*. 1964. Military account of the 1956 war.

2036 Bennett, Geoffrey. *Naval battles of the First World War*. 1968. The best one volume treatment.

2037 Bryant, Arthur. *The turn of the tide 1939—1943: a study based on the diaries and autobiographical notes of Field Marshal the Viscount Alanbrooke . . .* 1957. Continued in Bryant's *Triumph in the west*. New York, 1959. A significant but controversial treatment of grand strategy. Cf. (2044).

2038   Calvocoressi, Peter and Guy Wint. *Total war: causes and courses of the Second World War.* 1972. Good narrative.

2039   Carnegie Endowment for International Peace Series. *Economic and social history of the World War, British Series,* ed. James T. Shotwell. New Haven, Conn., 1921–40, 25 vols. For a complete listing of titles see (26). For individual items see (1494, 1509, 1546, 1593).

2040   Davin, Daniel M. *Crete* (New Zealand Official History). Oxford, 1953. Might well be supplemented by Stewart, I.McD.G. *The struggle for Crete, 20 May – 1 June 1941.* Oxford, 1966.

2041   Dunlop, John K. *The development of the British army, 1899–1914.* 1938.

2042   Higham, Robin D.S. *Armed forces in peace time: Britain, 1918–1940, a case study.* 1962.

2043   Holt, Edgar. *The Boer War.* 1958.

2044   Howard, Michael Eliot. *The Mediterranean strategy in the Second World War.* 1968. A brilliant critique of (2037).

2045   James, Robert Rhodes. *Gallipoli.* 1965. The best account. See also the classic, Moorehead, Alan. *Gallipoli.* 1956. And Hamilton, Ian, *Gallipoli Diary.* 1920, 2 vols. Hamilton was commander of allied forces until October 1915.

2046   Liddell Hart, Basil Henry. *A History of the World War 1914–1918.* 2nd ed., 1934. First published as *The real war 1914–1918.* 1930. Considered by many the best general history. For another excellent one-volume treatment see Falls, Cyril B. *The First World War.* 1960.

2047   —— *History of the Second World War.* 1970. Also excellent is Collier, Basil. *A short history of the Second World War.* New York, 1967.

2048   Marder, Arthur J. *From the dreadnought to Scapa Flow: the Royal Navy in the Fisher era, 1904–1919.* 1961–70, 5 vols.

2049   Mason, Francis K. *Battle over Britain.* New York, 1969. Another absorbing account is Collier, Basil. *The Battle of Britain.* 1962. Mason includes the air assaults of 1917–19 and the development of air defence between the wars. And see Wright, Robert. *Dowding and the Battle of Britain.* 1969. Dowding was commander-in-chief of Fighter Command.

2050   Official Histories: First World War, 1914–18

Military Operations

East Africa. Vol. 1, August 1914 – September 1916 (incomplete). By Charles Hordern. 1941.

Egypt and Palestine. By George MacMunn and Cyril B. Falls. 1928–30, 2 vols.

France and Belgium. By James E. Edmonds. 1922–49, 14 vols.

Italy, 1915–1919. By James E. Edmonds *et al.* 1949.

Macedonia. By Cyril Falls. 1933–5, 2 vols.

Mesopotamia. By Frederick J. Moberly. 1923–7, 4 vols.

Togoland and the Cameroons, 1914–16. By Frederick J. Moberly. 1931.

Order of Battle Divisions

Medical

Naval Operations

Corbett, Julian S. and Henry Newbolt. *History of the Great War: Naval operations.* 1920–31, 5 vols. Vol. III (including the Battle of Jutland), rev. ed., 1940.

Air Operations

Raleigh, Walter Alexander and H.A. Jones. *The war in the air.* Oxford, 1922–37, 6 vols.

2051   Official Histories: Second World War, 1939–45

United Kingdom Military Series. James R.M. Butler (ed.).

Grand Strategy

I. *1933 to September 1939.* (Not yet published.)

II. *September 1939 – June 1941.* By James R.M. Butler. 1957.

III. *June 1941 – August 1942.* By J.M.A. Gwyer and James R.M. Butler. 1964.

IV. *August 1942 – August 1943.* By Michael Howard. 1972.

V—VI. *August 1943 — August 1945.* By John Ehrman. 1956.
Campaigns
  The campaign in Norway. By T.K. Derry. 1952.
  France and Flanders, 1939—40. By L.F. Ellis. 1953.
  The Mediterranean and Middle East. By Ian Stanley Ord Playfair, C.J.C.
    Molony *et al.* 1954—73, 5 vols.
  The war against Japan. By S. Woodburn Kirby *et al.* 1957—69, 5 vols.
  Victory in the west. By L.F. Ellis *et al.* 1962, 2 vols.
  The defence of the United Kingdom. By Basil Collier. 1957.
  The strategic air offensive. By Charles Webster and Noble Frankland. 1961,
    4 vols.
  The war at sea, 1939—45. By Stephen W. Roskill. 1954—61, 3 vols. in 4.
  The Royal Air Force, 1939—45. By Denis Richards and Hilary St G. Saunders.
    1953—4, 3 vols.
United Kingdom Civil Series. William Keith Hancock (ed.).
  Introductory. This includes *Statistical digest of the war* (Central Statistical
    Office). 1951. See also (1302, 1579).
  General Series
  War Production Series
United Kingdom Medical Series. Arthur S. MacNalty (ed.).
2052   Roskill, Stephen W. *Naval policy between the wars*, I, *The period of Anglo-
        American antagonism 1919—1929.* 1968. Facile and thorough; excellent
        bibliography.
2053   —— *The strategy of sea power: its development and application.* 1962.
2054   Turner, Ernest S. *The phoney war.* New York, 1962. On events of 1939 and
        early 1940. In England published as *The phoney war on the home front.*
        1961.
2055   Woodward, Ernest Llewellyn. *Great Britain and the war of 1914—1918.* 1967.
        Excellent general account.

4 Biographies

2056   Callwell, C.E. *Field Marshal Sir Henry Wilson: his life and diaries.* 1927, 2
        vols. Wilson was chief of the Imperial Staff 1918—22. Especially useful
        for strategic problems. Cf. Terraine, John. *The western front 1914—1918.*
        1964.
2057   Chalmers, William S. *The life and letters of David, Earl Beatty.* 1951. Beatty,
        commander-in-chief of the Grand Fleet, 1916—19, was a key figure in the
        Battle of Jutland.
2058   Colville, John R. *Man of valour: the life of Field-Marshal, the Viscount Gort.*
        1972.
2059   Connell, John [John Henry Robertson]. *Auchinleck.* 1959.
2060   —— *Wavell, soldier and scholar to June 1941.* 1964.
2061   French, E. Gerald. *The life of Field-Marshal Sir John French, First Earl of
        Ypres.* 1931. As yet nothing better on French.
2062   Hannah, W.H. *Bobs: Kipling's general: life of Field Marshal Earl Roberts of
        Kandahar, V.C.* 1972.
2063   MacKay, Ruddock F. *Fisher of Kilverstone.* Oxford, 1974. The latest and one
        of the best biographies. For primary material see Marder, Arthur J. (ed.),
        *Fear God and dread nought: the correspondence of Admiral of the Fleet
        Lord Fisher of Kilverstone* (1952—9, 3 vols.), and Kemp, Peter K. (ed.),
        The papers of Admiral Sir John Fisher (1960—4, 2 vols.).
2064   Marder, Arthur J. *Portrait of an admiral: the life and papers of Sir Herbert
        Richmond.* 1952.
2065   Nicolson, Nigel. *Alex: the life of Field Marshal Earl Alexander of Tunis.*
        1973.
2066   Terraine, John. *Life and times of Lord Mountbatten.* 1968. In considerable
        part Mountbatten's own account.
2067   —— *Douglas Haig, the educated soldier.* 1963. There are earlier biographies
        by Duff Cooper (1935—6, 2 vols.) and by John Charteris (1929).

5 Articles

2068   Gibbs, Norman. 'British strategic doctrine, 1918—1939', in Howard, Michael
        E. (ed.). *The theory and practice of war: essays presented to Captain B.H.
        Liddell Hart on his seventieth birthday*. 1965, pp. 185—212.
2069   Howard, Michael E. 'Lord Haldane and the territorial army', in Howard's
        Studies in war and peace. 1970, pp. 83—98.
2070   Terraine, John. 'Twenty-five years of military history, 1945—1970', *Journal
        of the Royal United Services Institute for Defence Studies*, CXVI (Dec.
        1971), 13—23.

XIII. RELIGIOUS HISTORY

1 Printed sources

2071   Bayne, Stephen Fielding, Jr. *An Anglican turning point: documents and
        interpretations*. 1964. When Bayne was Executive Officer of the Anglican
        Communion, 1960—4.
2072   Bell, George K.A. (ed.). *Documents on Christian unity: a selection from the
        first and second series 1920—30*. 1955. See also Bell, G.K.A. (ed.), *Docu-
        ments on Christian unity, third series, 1930—1948*. 1948.
2073   Buchman, Frank N.D. *Remaking the world*. 1947. Speeches.
2074   *Conversations between the Church of England and the Methodist Church: a
        report to the Archbishops of Canterbury and York and the Conference of
        the Methodist Church*. 1963. Concerning union.
2075   COPEC. *Politics and citizenship, being the report presented to the Conference
        on Christian Politics, Economics and Citizenship at Birmingham, April 5—
        12, 1924*. 1925. See (2089).
2076   Edwards, David L. (ed.). *The Honest to God debate. Some reactions to the
        book 'Honest to God'*. Philadelphia, Pa., 1963. See (2095).
2077   Eliot, Thomas S. *Christianity and culture: the idea of a Christian society and
        notes towards the definition of culture*. New York [1940]. A widely dis-
        cussed book.
2078   Garbett, Cyril F. *In an age of revolution*. 1952. Concerning 1880—1950.
2079   Heenan, John C. *A crown of thorns: an autobiography, 1951—1963*. 1974.
        By the Archbishop of Westminster.
2080   —— *Not the whole truth*. 1971. The first volume of the autobiography. See
        also (2079).
2081   Henson, Herbert Hensley. *Retrospect of an unimportant life*. 1942—50, 3
        vols. Autobiography of the Bishop of Durham.
2082   Inge, William Ralph. *Diary of a dean: St Paul's 1911—1934*. New York, 1950.
2083   —— *Outspoken essays*. 1919. See also *Outspoken essays, second series*.
        1923. For commentary on Inge's thought, see Helm, Robert M. *The
        gloomy dean*. 1962.
2084   Lambeth Conference. *Conference of bishops of the Anglican communion:
        holden at Lambeth Palace . . . 1908. Encyclical letter from the bishops,
        with the resolutions and reports*. 1908.
2085   —— *The reports of the 1920, 1930 and 1948 conferences . . . 1948*.
2086   —— *Lambeth Conference 1948: the encyclical letter from the bishops;
        together with resolutions and reports*. 1948. A notable conference.
2087   Lewis, Clive S. *The screwtape letters*. 1942. A lay churchman on a theological
        theme.
2088   Lewis, W.H. (ed.). *Letters of C.S. Lewis*. New York, 1966. During the years
        1915—63. See also (2087).
2089   [Lindsay, Alexander D., Baron, ed.] . *Christianity and the present moral un-
        rest*. 1926. By various writers; inspired by COPEC. See (2075).
2090   *Malvern, 1941. The life of the church and the order of society; being the pro-
        ceedings of the Archbishop of York's Conference*. 1941.

2091   [Oldham, Joseph H.]. *The churches survey their task. The report of the con-ference at Oxford, July 1937 on church, community and state*. With an introduction by J.H. Oldham. 1937.
2092   Orchard, William E. *From faith to faith: an autobiography of religious devel-opment*. New York, 1933. Orchard was minister at the King's Weigh House, London.
2093   Pickering, William S.F. (ed.). *Anglican—Methodist relations: some insti-tutional factors*. Papers presented to the Study Commission on Insti-tutionalism, Commission on Faith and Order, World Council of Churches. 1961. Pertaining to the search for unity.
2094   Reckitt, Maurice B. *As it happened: an autobiography*. 1941.
2095   Robinson, John A.T. *Honest to God*. 1964. See (2076).
2096   Smethurst, Arthur F. (ed.). *Acts of the convocations of Canterbury and York together with certain other resolutions, passed since the reform of the convocations in 1921*. 1948.
2097   Smith, Warren Sylvester (ed.). *The religious speeches of Bernard Shaw*. Uni-versity Park, Pa., 1963. From 1906 to 1937.
2098   Southcott, Ernest W. *The parish comes alive*. New York, 1957. Evangelism in a parish over a period of twelve years.
2099   Temple, Frederick S. (ed.). *William Temple: some Lambeth letters*. 1963. 'Of a busy war-time archbishop, 1942—4.'
2100   Temple, William. *Christianity and the social order*. New York, 1942. When Temple was Archbishop of York.
2101   Underhill, Evelyn. *Mysticism: a study in the nature and development of man's spiritual consciousness*. 7th ed., 1918. Important book by a noted religious writer.
2102   —— *The life of the spirit and the life of today*. 1922.
2103   Weatherhead, Leslie D. *The Christian agnostic*. 1965. The minister (1936—60) of the City Temple, London, analyses his own faith.

2 Surveys

2104   Davies, Horton. *Worship and theology in England*, V, *The ecumenical century 1900—1965*. Princeton, N.J., 1965. Masterful treatment.
2105   Davies, Rupert E. *Methodism*. 1963.
2106   Headlam, Arthur C. *The Church of England*. 2nd ed., 1925.
2107   Jones, Robert Tudur. *Congregationalism in England, 1662—1962*. 1962.
2108   Lloyd, Roger. *The Church of England 1900—1965*. 1966. A revised edition of his *Church of England in the twentieth century*. 1946—50, 2 vols.
2109   Mathew, David. *Catholicism in England*. 3rd ed., 1955.
2110   Moorman, John R.H. *A history of the church in England*. Rev. ed., 1973.
2111   Neill, Stephen Charles. *Anglicanism*. 1958.
2112   Ramsey, Arthur Michael. *An era in Anglican theology from Gore to Temple: the development of Anglican theology between Lux Mundi and the Sec-ond World War, 1889—1939*. New York, 1960.
2113   Spinks, G. Stephens *et al. Religion in Britain since 1900*. 1952.
2114   Underwood, Alfred C. *A history of the English Baptists*. 1947.

3 Monographs

2115   *The City Temple in the City of London*. Published by the City Temple Church Council on the occasion of the reopening and rededication. 1958.
2116   Clark, Walter Houston. *The Oxford Group: its history and significance*. New York, 1951. A critical study of Moral Re-Armament.
2117   Clarke, W.K. Lowther. *A hundred years of hymns ancient and modern*. 1961.
2118   Craig, Robert. *Social concern in the thought of William Temple*. 1963.
2119   Crossman, Richard H.S. (ed.). *Oxford and the Groups*. Oxford, 1934.
2120   Cruickshank, Marjorie. *Church and state in English education, 1870 to the present day*. 1963.
2121   Cuming, Geoffrey J. *A history of Anglican liturgy*. 1969.

2122   Currie, Robert. *Methodism divided: a study in the sociology of ecumenical-ism.* 1968.

2123   Davies, Horton. *Varieties of English preaching, 1900–1960.* 1963.

2124   Driberg, Tom. *The mystery of moral rearmament: a study of Frank Buchman and his movement.* 1964.

2125   Edwards, David L. *Religion and change.* 1969.

2126   Edwards, Maldwyn. *Methodism and England: a study of Methodism in its social and political aspects 1850–1932.* 1943.

2127   Freeman, Ruth. *Quakers and peace.* 1947.

2128   Goodall, Norman. *A history of the London Missionary Society 1895–1945.* 1954.

2129   —— *Ecumenical progress: a decade of change in the ecumenical movement 1961–71.* 1972.

2130   Hickey, John. *Urban Catholics: urban Catholicism in England and Wales from 1829 to the present day.* 1967.

2131   Kaye, Elaine. *The history of the King's Weigh House.* 1968. An Anglican church become Congregational.

2132   Kissack, Reginald. *Church or no church? A study of the development of the concept of Church in British Methodism.* 1964.

2133   Langford, Thomas A. *In search of foundations: English theology 1900–1920.* Nashville, Tenn., 1969.

2134   Lewis, John *et al.* (eds.). *Christianity and the social revolution.* New York, 1936. Various authors challenge the 'traditional attitudes of Christianity towards . . . radical social change'. (Preface.)

2135   Major, Henry D.A. *English modernism: its origins, methods, aims.* 1927.

2136   Marrin, Albert. *The last crusade: the Church of England in the First World War.* Durham, N.C., 1974. A scholarly study, relying largely on printed sources.

2137   Mayfield, Guy. *The Church of England: its members and its business.* 1963.

2138   Mozley, John Kenneth. *Some tendencies in British theology. From the publication of 'Lux Mundi' to the present day.* 1951.

2139   Neill, Stephen Charles. *A history of Christian missions.* 1965.

2140   —— *The interpretation of the New Testament, 1861–1961.* 1964. Based on the Firth Lectures at Nottingham in 1962.

2141   —— *Towards Church union 1937–1952.* 1952. On this question, there are, after 1952, summaries twice annually by J.R. Nelson in the *Ecumenical Review.*

2142   Nuttall, Geoffrey F. and Owen Chadwick (eds.). *From uniformity to unity 1662–1962.* 1962. Includes essays on twentieth century by Oliver S. Tomkins and John Huxtable.

2143   Oliver, John. *The church and social order: social thought in the Church of England, 1918–1939.* 1968. A significant book with useful bibliography.

2144   Page, Robert J. *New directions in Anglican theology: a survey from Temple to Robinson.* New York, 1965.

2145   Payne, Ernest A. *The Baptist Union: a short history.* 1959.

2146   Reckitt, Maurice B. (ed.). *For Christ and the people: studies of four socialist priests and prophets of the Church of England between 1870 and 1930.* 1968. Analyses of Thomas Hancock, Stewart Headlam, Charles Marson and Conrad Noel.

2147   —— *Maurice to Temple. A Century of the Social Movement in the Church of England.* 1947. On period 1846–1946.

2148   —— (ed.). *Prospect for Christianity: essays in Catholic social reconstruction.* 1945.

2149   Rouse, Ruth and Stephen Charles Neill (eds.). *A history of the ecumenical movement 1517–1948.* 2nd ed., Philadelphia, Pa., 1968. A standard work. Continued by Harold E. Fey (ed.), *Ecumenical advance: a history of the ecumenical movement,* II, *1948–1968.* Philadelphia, Pa., 1970.

2150   Sacks, Benjamin. *The religious issue in the state schools of England and Wales, 1902–1914.* Albuquerque, New Mexico, 1961.

2151   Sails, George W. *At the centre: the story of Methodism's central missions.* 1970.

RELIGIOUS HISTORY

2152 Thompson, Kenneth A. *Bureaucracy and church reform: the organizational response of the Church of England to social change, 1800—1965.* Oxford, 1970.
2153 Vidler, Alec R. *The modernist movement in the Roman Church; its origins and outcome.* Cambridge, 1934. Much reference to Great Britain.
2154 —— *20th century defenders of the faith.* 1965. Robertson lectures at the University of Glasgow, 1964.
2155 Warren, Max. *The missionary movement from Britain in modern history.* 1965.
2156 Wearmouth, Robert F. *Methodism and the trade unions.* 1959.
2157 —— *The social and political influence of Methodism in the twentieth century.* 1957. An admirable study.
2158 Wiggins, Arch A. *The history of the Salvation Army,* V, *1904—1914.* 1968.
2159 Williams, Daniel Day. *What present-day theologians are thinking.* 3rd ed., rev., New York, 1967.
2160 Williams, Geoffrey. *Inside Buchmanism: an independent inquiry into the Oxford Group movement and Moral Rearmament.* 1955.
2161 Wilson, Roger C. *Quaker relief. An Account of the relief work of the Society of Friends, 1940—1948.* 1952.
2162 Wood, Herbert George. *Living issues in religious thought from George Fox to Bertrand Russell.* Freeport, N.Y., 1966. First published in 1924; includes religious views of Russell, Bernard Shaw and H.G. Wells.
2163 Young, Kenneth. *Chapel: the joyous days and prayerful nights of the non-conformists in their heyday, circa 1850—1950.* 1972. Largely derived from 'the memories' of those who wrote the author.

4 Biographies

2164 [Barnett, Henrietta Octavia]. *Canon Barnett, his life, work and friends.* By his wife. 1918, 2 vols. Biography of Samuel Augustus Barnett, 1844—1913.
2165 Bell, George K.A. *Randall Davidson, Archbishop of Canterbury.* 3rd ed., 1952.
2166 Carpenter, Spencer C. *Winnington-Ingram: the biography of Arthur Foley Winnington-Ingram, Bishop of London 1901—1939.* 1949.
2167 —— *Duncan-Jones of Chichester.* 1956.
2168 Cropper, Margaret. *Evelyn Underhill.* 1958.
2169 Edwards, David L. *Leaders of the Church of England, 1828—1944.* 1971.
2170 —— *Ian Ramsey, Bishop of Durham: a memoir.* Oxford, 1973.
2171 Fletcher, Joseph. *William Temple: twentieth century Christian.* 1963. 'A portrait.'
2172 Fox, Adam. *Dean Inge.* 1960.
2173 Gordon, Anne Wolrige. *Peter Howard: life and letters.* 1969. Howard was a leader in Moral Rearmament.
2174 Heenan, John C. *Cardinal Hinsley.* 1944.
2175 Iremonger, Frederic A. *William Temple, Archbishop of Canterbury: his life and letters.* 1948.
2176 Jasper, Ronald. *Arthur Cayley Headlam: life and letters of a bishop.* 1960. Headlam was Bishop of Gloucester 1923—45.
2177 —— *George Bell, Bishop of Chichester.* 1967.
2178 Kemp, Eric Waldram. *Life and letters of Kenneth Escott Kirk, Bishop of Oxford 1937—1954.* 1959.
2179 Lockhart, John G. *Cosmo Gordon Lang.* 1949. Biography of the Archbishop of Canterbury, 1928—42.
2180 McKay, Roy. *John Leonard Wilson, confessor for the faith.* 1973. Biography of the Bishop of Birmingham, 1953—69.
2181 Maitland, Christopher. *Dr Leslie Weatherhead of the City Temple.* 1960.
2182 [Margaret], the Prioress of Whitby. *Archbishop Garbett: a memoir.* 1957.
2183 Paget, Stephen. *Henry Scott Holland, memoir and letters.* 1921. Biography of a Regius Professor of Divinity at Oxford.

2184   Prestige, George L. *The life of Charles Gore, a great Englishman*. 1935. Gore was Bishop of Birmingham and Bishop of Oxford.
2185   Reckitt, Maurice B. *P.E.T. Widdrington, a study in vocation and versatility*. 1961. Study of a key figure in the Anglo-Catholic movement.
2186   Roberts, Richard Ellis. *H.R.L. Sheppard: life and letters*. 1942. Study of a noted vicar of St Martin-in-the-Fields and dean of Canterbury.
2187   Smyth, Charles. *Cyril Forster Garbett, archbishop of York*. 1959.
2188   Tomkins, Oliver. *The life of Edward Woods*. 1957. Biography of the bishop of Lichfield, associated with the Life and Liberty Movement.
2189   Wakefield, Gordon S. *Robert Newton Flew, 1886–1962*. 1971. Biography of a leading Methodist.
2190   Wood, Herbert George. *Henry T. Hodgkin, a memoir*. 1937. A study of a leader in the Fellowship of Reconciliation.
2191   Woods, Edward S. and Frederic B. MacNutt. *Theodore, Bishop of Winchester*. 1933. Biography of F.T. Woods.

5 Articles

2192   Brown, L.W. *et al.* 'Anglican–Methodist unity: a symposium', *The Church Quarterly*, I (Oct. 1968), 98–136. Subject: the report of the Anglican–Methodist Unity Commission.
2193   Cannon, Charmian. 'The influence of religion on educational policy, 1902–1944', *BJES*, XII (May 1964), 143–60.
2194   Cline, Catherine Ann. 'The Church and the movement for Congo Reform', *Church History*, XXXII (Mar. 1963), 46–56.
2195   Edwards, David L. '101 years of the Lambeth Conference', *The Church Quarterly*, I (July 1968), 21–35.
2196   Finlay, John L. 'The religious response to Douglasism in England', *Journal of Religious History*, VI (Dec. 1971), 363–83. On Major C.H. Douglas and Social Credit.
2197   Fuller, Reginald H. 'Draft liturgy of 1953 in Anglican perspective', *Anglican Theological Review*, XLI (July 1959), 190–8.
2198   Hachey, Thomas E. 'The archbishop of Canterbury's visit to Palestine: an issue in Anglo-Vatican relations in 1931', *Church History*, XLI (June 1972), 198–207. Uses Foreign Office papers.
2199   Hill, Clifford. 'From church to sect: West Indian religious sect development in Britain', *Journal for the Scientific Study of Religion*, X (Summer, 1971), 114–23. Studies the period 1951–71.
2200   Langford, Thomas A. 'The theological methodology of John Oman and H.H. Farmer', *Religious Studies*, I (1965–6), 229–40.
2201   Morgan, D.H.J. 'The social and educational background of Anglican bishops – continuities and changes', *BJS*, XX (Sept. 1969), 295–310.
2202   Nichols, James Hastings. 'Religion in Toynbee's history', *Journal of Religion*, XXVIII (Jan. 1948), 99–119.
2203   Pugh, D.R. 'The Church and education: Anglican attitudes, 1902', *Journal of Ecclesiastical History*, XXIII (July 1972), 219–32.
2204   Smith, Bardwell L. 'Liberal Catholicism: an Anglican perspective', *Anglican Theological Review*, LIV (July 1972), 175–93. On period 1889–1914.

XIV. HISTORY OF THE FINE ARTS

1 Printed sources

2205   Beecham, Thomas. *A mingled chime: an autobiography*. New York, 1943.
2206   Dolmetsch, Mabel. *Personal recollections of Arnold Dolmetsch*. 1957. Concerning a noted musicologist.
2207   Fellowes, Edmund H. *Memoirs of an amateur musician*. 1946.
2208   Gill, Eric. *Autobiography*. 1940. Of a notable stone carver.

2209 Holst, Imogen. *The music of Gustav Holst*. 2nd ed., 1968.
2210 Howes, Frank Stewart. *The music of Ralph Vaughan Williams*. 1954.
2211 James, Philip (ed.). *Henry Moore on sculpture: a collection of the sculptor's writings and spoken words*. Rev. ed., New York, 1971.
2212 Jekyll, Gertrude. *Colour schemes for the flower garden*. 8th ed., 1936.
2213 —— and Christopher Hussey. *Garden ornament*. 2nd ed., 1927.
2214 —— and Lawrence Weaver. *Gardens for small country houses*. 6th ed., 1927.
2215 Rothenstein, John. *Brave day, hideous night. Summer's lease. Time's thievish progress*. 1965—70, 3 vols. Autobiography of the director of the Tate Gallery, 1938—64.
2216 Rothenstein, William. *Men and memories: recollections of William Rothenstein*. 1931—2, 2 vols. Vol. II embraces 1900—22.
2217 Scott, M.H. Baillie and A. Edgar Beresford. *Houses and Gardens*. 1939.
2218 Shewring, Walter (ed.). *Letters of Eric Gill*. 1947.
2219 Sickert, Walter. *A free house! Or the artist as craftsman*, ed. Osbert Sitwell. 1947. The writings of Sickert.

2 Surveys

2220 Cooper, Martin (ed.). *The new Oxford history of music*, X, *The modern age 1890—1960*. Oxford, 1974.
2221 Gaunt, William. *A concise history of English painting*. 1964.
2222 Goodhart-Rendel, Harry S. *English architecture since the regency: an interpretation*. 1953.
2223 Hitchcock, Henry-Russell. *Architecture: nineteenth and twentieth centuries*. 3rd ed., 1968.
2224 Howes, Frank. *The English musical renaissance*. 1966. Nineteenth and twentieth centuries.
2225 Mackerness, Eric D. *A social history of English music*. 1964.
2226 Myers, Rollo H. *Twentieth century music*. 2nd ed., 1968.
2227 Richards, James M. *An introduction to modern architecture*. 1940.
2228 Walker, Ernest. *A history of music in England*. 3rd ed. rev. by J.A. Westrup. Oxford, 1952. Standard.
2229 Wilson, Albert E. *Edwardian theatre*. 1951.
2230 Young, Percy M. *A history of British music*. 1967.

3 Monographs

2231 The Arts Enquiry. *Music: a report on musical life in England sponsored by the Dartington Hall trustees*. 1949. PEP publication, see (108).
2232 Arundell, Dennis. *The story of Sadler's Wells, 1683—1964*. 1965.
2233 Barman, Christian. *An introduction to railway architecture*. 1950.
2234 Butler, Arthur S.G. *The architecture of Sir Edwin Lutyens*. 1950, 3 vols.
2235 Chadwick, George F. *The park and the town: public landscape in the 19th and 20th centuries*. New York, 1966. Excellent treatment, with emphasis on Britain.
2236 Clarke, Mary. *The Sadler's Wells ballet: a history and an appreciation*. 1955.
2237 Colles, Henry C. *The Royal College of Music: a jubilee record, 1883—1933*. 1933.
2238 Crowe, Sylvia. *Garden design*. 1958.
2239 Dannatt, Trevor. *Modern architecture in Britain: selected examples of recent building*. 1959.
2240 Dent, Edward J. *A theatre for everybody: the story of the Old Vic and Sadler's Wells*. 1945. A popular, well-informed treatment.
2241 Dickinson, Alan E.F. *Vaughan Williams*. 1963. A study of his compositions.
2242 Foss, Hubert. *Ralph Vaughan Williams: a study*. 1950.
2243 Gelatt, Roland. *The fabulous phonograph: the story of the gramophone from tin foil to high fidelity*. 1956.
2244 Godfrey, W.G. *The work of Ernest Newton, R.A.* 1923.
2245 Grigoriev, Sergi L. *The Diaghilev Ballet, 1909—1929*. 1953.

2246 Harris, John S. *Government patronage of the arts in Great Britain.* Chicago, 1970. After 1945.
2247 Hill, Ralph. *Music.* 1950. Developments after 1945.
2248 Hinchcliffe, Arnold P. *British Theatre, 1950—1970.* Oxford, 1974.
2249 Howarth, Thomas. *Charles Rennie Mackintosh and the modern movement.* 1952. Architecture.
2250 Kaye, Barrington. *The development of the architectural profession in Britain: a sociological study.* 1960.
2251 Kemp, Thomas C. and John C. Trewin. *The Stratford Festival: a history of the Shakespeare Memorial Theatre.* Birmingham, 1953.
2252 Kennedy, Michael. *History of the Royal Manchester College of Music, 1893—1972.* Manchester, 1971.
2253 —— *The works of Ralph Vaughan Williams.* 1964.
2254 King, A. Hyatt. *Some British collectors of music, c. 1600—1960.* Cambridge, 1963.
2255 Melly, George. *Revolt into style: the pop arts in Britain.* 1970.
2256 Mitchell, Donald and Hans Keller (eds.). *Benjamin Britten: a commentary on his works from a group of specialists.* 1952.
2257 Nettel, Reginald. *The orchestra in England: a social history.* [1946.]
2258 Newton, Ernest and W.G. Newton. *English domestic architecture,* VI. n.d.
2259 Pakenham, Simona. *Ralph Vaughan Williams. A discovery of his music.* 1957. For the uninitiated.
2260 Pevsner, Nikolaus (ed.). *The buildings of England.* Harmondsworth, 1951—74. 46 vols. By counties: this celebrated work has just been completed.
2261 —— *Pioneers of modern design: from William Morris to Walter Gropius.* 2nd ed., 1966. Well illustrated chapter on English architecture.
2262 Richards, James M. (ed.). *The bombed buildings of Britain.* 3rd ed., 1947. 'A record of architectural casualties 1940—1.'
2263 Rosenthal, Harold. *Opera at Covent Garden: a short history.* 1967. Largely on twentieth century.
2264 Rothenstein, John. *British art since 1900; an anthology.* 1962.
2265 Royal Society of Arts. *A century of British progress 1851—1951.* 1951. Six papers read before the Royal Society in 1951.
2266 Royal Society of Arts. *The post-war home: a series of lectures on its interior and equipment.* Foreword by Oliver Lyttleton. 1942. Lectures delivered 1941—2.
2267 Scholes, Percy A. *The mirror of music, 1844—1944: a century of musical life as reflected in the pages of the 'Musical Times'.* 1947, 2 vols. Packed with information.
2268 Spence, Basil. *Phoenix at Coventry: the building of a cathedral.* 1962.
2269 Trewin, John C. *The Birmingham Repertory Theatre 1913—1963.* 1963.
2270 —— *Drama in Britain 1951—1964.* 1965. Continues (2271).
2271 —— *The theatre since 1900.* 1951. Continued in (2270).
2272 Weaver, Lawrence. *Lutyens houses and gardens.* 1921. This is a new edition of Edwin L. Lutyens, *Houses and gardens.* 1913.
2273 —— *Small country houses of to-day.* [1910].
2274 Williamson, Audrey. *Ballet of 3 decades.* 1958. On period 1931—57.

4 Biographies

2275 Bailey, Cyril. *Hugh Percy Allen.* 1948. Biography of a musician and a musical statesman.
2276 Colles, Henry C. *Walford Davies: a biography.* 1942.
2277 Day, James. *Vaughan Williams.* 1961.
2278 Emmons, Robert. *The life and opinions of Walter Richard Sickert.* 1941.
2279 Fox Strangways, A.H. and Maud Karpeles. *Cecil Sharp.* 2nd ed., 1955. Biography of a collector and arranger of folk songs.
2280 Grierson, Mary. *Donald Francis Tovey: a biography based on letters.* 1952. Tovey was a leading musician and musicologist.
2281 Hall, Donald. *Henry Moore; the life and work of a great sculptor.* New York, 1966.

2282   Hassall, Christopher. *Edward Marsh, patron of the arts: a biography*. 1959.
2283   Hill, William Thompson. *Octavia Hill: pioneer of the National Trust and housing reformer*. 1956.
2284   Holst, Imogen. *Gustav Holst: a biography*. 2nd ed., 1969.
2285   Hussey, Christopher. *The life of Sir Edwin Lutyens*. 1950.
2286   Hutchings, Arthur. *Delius*. 1948.
2287   Kennedy, Michael. *Portrait of Elgar*. 1968.
2288   Kornwolf, James D. *M.H. Baillie Scott and the Arts and Crafts Movement; pioneers of modern design*. 1972.
2289   Laughton, Bruce. *Philip Wilson Steer 1860–1942*. Oxford, 1971.
2290   Lilly, Marjorie. *Sickert: the painter and his circle*. 1971.
2291   Massingham, Betty. *Miss Jekyll, portrait of a great gardener*. 1966.
2292   Pound, Reginald. *Sir Henry Wood*. 1969.
2293   Powell, Dora M. *Edward Elgar: memories of a variation*. 3rd ed., 1949.
2294   Reid, Charles. *Thomas Beecham: an independent biography*. 1961.
2295   Rothenstein, John. *The life and death of Conder*. 1938. On Charles Conder, a painter.
2296   St John, Christopher. *Ethel Smyth: a biography*. 1959.
2297   Speaight, Robert. *The life of Eric Gill*. 1966.
2298   —— *William Rothenstein: the portrait of an artist in his time*. 1962.
2299   Trewin, John C. *Benson and the Bensonians*. 1960. On Frank Benson (1858–1939), an actor.
2300   —— *Peter Brock: a biography*. 1971.
2301   —— *Robert Donat: a biography*. 1968.
2302   White, Eric Walter. *Benjamin Britten: his life and operas*. New ed., 1970.
2303   Whittick, Arnold. *Eric Mendelsohn*. 2nd ed., 1956. Ch. 6 concerns this architect's English phase, 1933–37.

5 Articles

2304   Antcliffe, Herbert. 'Problems of music and history', *Music & Letters*, IX (July 1928), 265–75.
2305   Foss, Hubert J. 'Elgar and his age', *Music & Letters*, XVI (Jan. 1935), 5–12.
2306   Fox Strangways, A.H. 'Ralph Vaughan Williams', *Music & Letters*, I (Apr. 1920), 78–86.
2307   King, A. Hyatt. 'The Forsytes and music', *Music & Letters*, XXIII (Jan. 1942), 24–36.
2308   Lethaby. 'William Richard Lethaby, 1857–1931, a symposium in honour of his centenary', *Journal of the Royal Institute of British Architects*, LXIV (1957), 218–25.
2309   Lovell, Percy. 'The proposed National Opera House at Glastonbury, 1913–15', *Music & Letters*, L (Jan. 1969), 172–9.
2310   'The music boom'; 'the musical balance sheet', *Economist*, CLII (Jan. 11 and 18, 1947), 53, 94–5.
2311   Pevsner, Nikolaus. 'Thoughts on Henry Moore', *Burlington Magazine*, LXXXVI (Feb. 1945), 47–9.

XV. INTELLECTUAL HISTORY

1 Printed sources
(See also sec. XI, pt. 1 and sec. XIII, pt. 1, above.)

2312   Angell, Norman. *After all*. New York [1951]. Autobiography.
2313   Ayerst, David (ed.). *The Guardian omnibus 1821–1971*. 1973. An anthology, largely twentieth century.
2314   Blumenfeld, Ralph D. *R.D.B's Diary, 1887–1914*. 1930.
2315   Bowra, Cecil Maurice. *Memories 1898–1939*. 1966. Of a classical scholar.
2316   Brittain, Vera. *Testament of youth: an autobiographical study of the years 1900–1925*. New York, 1933. Widely read in the thirties.

2317   Collingwood, Robin G. *An Autobiography*. 1938. Largely concerned with his studies in philosophy and history.
2318   Cornelius, David K. and Edwin St Vincent (eds.). *Cultures in conflict: perspectives on the Snow—Leavis controversy*. Chicago, 1964. Readings. See (2352).
2319   Coulton, George G. *Fourscore years: an autobiography*. 1944. By a leading historian and educationist.
2320   Day Lewis, Cecil. *The mind in chains: Socialism and the cultural revolution*. 1937. Essays on a revolutionary theme.
2321   Flexner, Abraham. *Universities: American—English—German*. 1930. An important book reflecting the ideas of its time.
2322   Gardiner, Alfred G. *Pillars of society*. 1913. See also his *Prophets, priests and kings*. 1914. Both are selections from Gardiner's writings in the *Daily News*.
2323   Harris, Henry Wilson. *Life so far*. 1954. Autobiography of a journalist and politician.
2324   *Higher education . . . report of the committee . . . under the chairmanship of Lord Robbins . . .* 1963. Cmnd 2154.
2325   Hirst, Francis W. *In the golden days*. 1947. Autobiography of the editor of the *Economist, 1907—1916*.
2326   Hobhouse, Leonard T. *Democracy and Reaction*. 1904. See also his *Liberalism*. 1911. These two works were widely read.
2327   Hobson, John A. *Confessions of an economic heretic*. 1938. Autobiography of a noted economist and publicist.
2328   —— *Imperialism: a study*. New York, 1902. Often considered Hobson's most influential book.
2329   Holmes—Laski letters. *The correspondence of Mr Justice Holmes and Harold J. Laski 1916—1935*, ed. Mark DeWolfe Howe. Cambridge, Mass., 1953, 2 vols.
2330   Jerrold, Douglas. *Georgian adventure*. New York, 1938. 'Memories' of an author and publisher.
2331   Joad, Cyril E.M. *Under the fifth rib: a belligerent autobiography*. 1932. By a writer, philosopher and teacher.
2332   Jones, Roderick. *A life in Reuters*. 1951.
2333   Keynes, John Maynard. *Two memoirs. Dr Melchier: a defeated enemy and my early beliefs*. 1949.
2334   Lehmann, John. *I am my brother*. 1960. Autobiographical; on World War II years.
2335   Mallock, William H. *Social reform as related to realities and delusions; an examination of the increase and distribution of wealth from 1801 to 1910*. 1914. An influential book.
2336   Marsh, Edward. *A number of people: a book of reminiscences*. 1939.
2337   Martin, Kingsley. *Father figures: a first volume of autobiography 1897—1931*. 1966. Continued by *Editor: a second volume of autobiography 1931—1945*. 1968. By the editor of the *New Statesman and Nation*, 1930—60.
2338   Massingham, Harold J. (ed.). *H.W.M.: a selection from the writings of H.W. Massingham*. 1925. Introduced by essays by J.L. Hammond, H.N. Brailsford, H.M. Tomlinson, H.W. Nevinson, Vaughan Nash and G. Bernard Shaw. Massingham was editor of the *Nation*, 1907—23. See (2458).
2339   Masterman, Charles F.G. *In peril of change*. 1905. See also (1215—16).
2340   Moore, George Edward. *The philosophy of G.E. Moore*, ed. Paul Arthur Schilpp, *Library of Living Philosophers*, Vol. IV. Chicago 1942. See also Moore's *Principia ethica* (1909), widely read by intellectuals in the Edwardian period.
2341   Murray, Gilbert. *An unfinished autobiography with contributions by his friends*, ed. Jean Smith and Arnold Toynbee. 1960.
2342   Nevinson, Henry W. *More changes, more chances*. 1925. Autobiography, 1903—14, of a distinguished essayist and war correspondent. Concluded to 1926 by his *Last changes, last chances*. 1928.
2343   Oxford University. *Report of Commission of Inquiry*. 1966, 2 vols. The commission was headed by Lord Franks.

INTELLECTUAL HISTORY

2344 Political and Economic Planning. *Report on the British press: a survey of its current operations and problems with special reference to national newspapers and their part in public affairs.* 1938.

2345 *Royal Commission on the press, 1947—1949; report presented to Parliament by command of His Majesty June 1949.* Cmnd 7700.

2346 Russell, Bertrand. *Autobiography of Bertrand Russell.* 1967—9, 3 vols.

2347 —— *Philosophy.* New York, 1927. Published in England as *An outline of philosophy.* 1927.

2348 Selver, Paul. *Orage and the New Age circle: reminiscences and reflections.* 1959.

2349 Shaw, George Bernard. *Bernard Shaw, collected letters,* II, *1898—1910,* ed. Dan H. Laurence. 1972.

2350 —— *What I really wrote about the war.* New York, 1931.

2351 Sitwell, Osbert. *Laughter in the next room.* Boston, 1948. Includes important reflections on society, 1918—40.

2352 Snow, Charles Percy, Baron. *The two cultures and the scientific revolution.* 1961. A discussion of the harmony (or lack of it) between letters and science is continued in *The two cultures and a second look.* 1964. See comment by F.R. Leavis, *Two cultures?: the significance of C.P. Snow.* 1962. See also (2318).

2353 Spender, John A. *Life, journalism and politics.* New York, n.d., 2 vols. Spender was editor of the *Westminster Gazette,* 1896—1922. And see (2457).

2354 Spender, Stephen. *World within world.* 1951. Autobiography of a poet; political as well as literary.

2355 Strachey, Lytton. *Eminent Victorians.* 1918. Tells us more about the twentieth century than the nineteenth.

2356 Toynbee, Arnold. *Experiences.* 1969.

2357 Wells, Herbert G. *Experiment in autobiography.* New York, 1934.

2358 —— *Mr Britling sees it through.* 1916. This novel reflects Wells' own thoughts on World War I; a best seller in Great Britain and the United States.

2359 Whitehead, Alfred North and Bertrand Russell. *Principia mathematica.* 1910—13, 3 vols. One of the great works of the century.

2360 Williams, Francis. *Nothing so strange.* 1970. Autobiography of a journalist.

2361 Woodward, Ernest Llewellyn. *Short journey.* 1942. Memoirs (to 1939) of a historian.

2362 Woolf, Leonard. *Sowing.* 1960. *Growing.* 1961. *Beginning again.* 1964. *Downhill all the way.* 1967. *The journey not the arrival matters.* 1969. Autobiography of a noted writer and publicist.

2 Surveys

2363 Cox, Charles Brian and A.E. Dyson (eds.). *The twentieth-century mind: history, ideas and literature in Britain.* 1972, 3 vols. Useful essays by various writers.

2364 Hynes, Samuel L. *The Edwardian turn of mind.* Princeton, N.J., 1968. An important contribution.

2365 Scott-James, Rolfe A. *Fifty years of English literature 1900—1950, with a postscript, 1951 to 1955.* New ed., 1956. Excellent survey.

2366 Symons, Julian. *The thirties: a dream revolved.* 1960.

2367 Ward, Alfred Charles. *Twentieth century literature, 1901—1950.* 1956.

3 Monographs
(See also sec. XI, pt. 3 and sec. XIII, pt. 3, above.)

2368 Ashby, Eric and Mary Anderson. *The rise of the student estate in Britain.* 1970. On the student role in management of universities.

2369 Ashley, Maurice. *Churchill as historian.* 1968.

2370 Ausubel, Herman and J. Bartlet Brebner and Erling M. Hunt (eds.). *Some modern historians of Britain: essays in honor of R.L. Schuyler*. New York, 1951.

2371   Ayerst, David. *The Manchester Guardian: biography of a newspaper*. Ithaca, N.Y., 1971.
2372   Berdahl, Robert O. *British universities and the state*. Berkeley, Cal., 1959.
2373   *The Bibliographical Society 1892—1942: studies in retrospect*. 1945.
2374   *The British Press*. 1971. Prepared by Reference Division, Central Office of Information, London. Brief analysis with historical reference.
2375   Cantor, Leonard M. and I. Francis Roberts. *Further education in England and Wales*. 1969. Other than universities and colleges of education.
2376   Carter, John. *Taste and technique in book-collecting: a study of recent developments in Great Britain and the United States*. New York, 1970.
2377   Chapman, Arthur William. *The story of a modern university: a history of the University of Sheffield*. 1955.
2378   Charlton, Henry B. *Portrait of a university 1851—1951*. Manchester, 1951. History of the University of Manchester.
2379   Clark, Ronald W. *A biography of the Nuffield Foundation*. 1972.
2380   Cole, George D.H. *A history of socialist thought*. 1953—60, 5 vols. Vols 3—5 concern Great Britain in the twentieth century down to 1939.
2381   Craik, William W. *The Central Labour College 1909—29: a chapter in the history of adult working-class education*. 1964.
2382   Deane, Herbert A. *The political ideas of Harold Laski*. New York, 1955.
2383   Dent, Harold Collett. *Universities in transition*. 1961. On period 1939—60.
2384   *The Economist, 1843—1943: a centenary volume*. 1943. Essays.
2385   Elton, Godfrey, Baron (ed.). *The first fifty years of the Rhodes Trust and the Rhodes scholarships, 1903—53*. 1955.
2386   Fyfe, Henry Hamilton. *Sixty years of Fleet Street*. 1949. Anecdotal.
2387   Gallie, Walter B. *A new university: A.D. Lindsay and the Keele experiment*. 1960.
2388   Ginsberg, Morris (ed.). *Law and opinion in England in the 20th century*. 1959. Text of 17 public lectures at the London School of Economics, 1957—8.
2389   Glass, Stanley T. *The responsible society: the ideas of the English Guild Socialist*. 1966.
2390   Gollin, Alfred M. *The Observer and J.L. Garvin 1908—1914: a study in a great editorship*. 1960.
2391   Greenberger, Allen J. *The British image of India: a study in the literature of imperialism 1880—1960*. 1969.
2392   Gross, John. *The rise and fall of the man of letters*. 1969.
2393   Halsey, Albert H. and M.A. Trow. *The British academics*. Cambridge, Mass., 1971. Evolution of the academic profession; highly statistical.
2394   Hardy, Godfrey H. *Bertrand Russell and Trinity*. Cambridge, 1970.
2395   Harrison, John F.C. *Learning and living, 1790—1960: a study in the history of the English adult education movement*. 1961.
2396   Heindel, Richard H. *The American impact on Great Britain, 1898—1914*. Philadelphia, Pa., 1940.
2397   *The Historical Association, 1906—1956*. 1955. Brief, informative account.
2398   *History of The Times*, III, *The twentieth century test 1884—1912*. 1947. IV, *The 150th anniversary and beyond, 1912—1948*. 1952, 2 vols.
2399   Howard, Michael S. *Jonathan Cape, publisher*. 1971. A history.
2400   Hutchison, Sidney C. *The history of the Royal Academy, 1768—1968*. 1968.
2401   Hyams, Edward. *The New Statesman: the history of the first fifty years 1913—1963*. 1963.
2402   Jackson, Ian. *The provincial press and the community*. Manchester 1971.
2403   Johnstone, John K. *The Bloomsbury group: a study of E.M. Forster, Lytton Strachey, Virginia Woolf and their circle*. 1954. A considerable bibliography concerning this 'circle' has accumulated, including Michael Holroyd, *Lytton Strachey: a critical biography* (1967—8, 2 vols) and Quentin Bell, *Virginia Woolf: a biography* (1972).
2404   Kelly, Thomas. *A history of adult education in Great Britain*. 2nd ed., Liverpool, 1970.

2405 —— *A history of public libraries in Great Britain 1845–1965.* 1973.
2406 Kingsford, Reginald J.L. *The Publishers Association, 1896–1946.* Cambridge, 1970.
2407 Knickerbocker, Frances Wentworth. *Free minds: John Morley and his friends.* 1943.
2408 Martin, Wallace. *The 'New Age' under Orage; chapters in English cultural history.* Manchester, 1967.
2409 Maude, Angus. *The common problem.* 1969. Examination of modern economics and sociology.
2410 Miller, Edward. *That noble cabinet: a history of the British Museum.* 1973.
2411 Minto, John. *A history of the public library movement in Great Britain and Ireland.* 1932.
2412 Mitchell, G. Duncan. *A hundred years of sociology.* 1968.
2413 Moody, Theodore and James C. Beckett. *Queen's, Belfast, 1845–1949: the history of a university.* 1959, 2 vols.
2414 Mountford, James. *British universities.* 1966.
2415 Mumby, Frank and Ian Norris. *Bookselling and book publishing: a history from the earliest times to the present day.* 5th ed., 1974.
2416 Murray, George. *The press and the public: the story of the British Press Council.* Carbindale, Ill., 1972. Since its inception in 1953.
2417 Panichas, George A. (ed.). *Promise of greatness, the war of 1914–1918.* 1968. Comment and reminiscence (literary, political, social) from a wide selection of writers including Blunden, Graves and Liddell Hart.
2418 Partridge, Eric and John W. Clark. *British and American English since 1900.* New York, 1951. *The only significant treatment of language change.*
2419 Passmore, John. *A hundred years of philosophy.* 2nd ed., 1966.
2420 [Pope, Wilson *et al.*]. *The story of 'The Star', 1888–1938.* [1938].
2421 Porter, Bernard. *Critics of empire: British radical attitudes to colonialism in Africa, 1895–1914.* 1968.
2422 Pound, Reginald. *The Strand Magazine, 1891–1950.* 1966.
2423 Robertson, William. *Welfare in trust: a history of the Carnegie United Kingdom Trust, 1913–1963.* Dunfermline, 1964.
2424 Royal Society. *Notes and records of the Royal Society of London.* Vol. I–. 1938–. Semi-annual. Notes of society's activities; articles on history of science.
2425 Scott, George. *Reporter anonymous: the story of the Press Association.* 1968.
2426 Shackle, George L.S. *The years of high theory: invention and tradition in economic thought, 1926–1939.* Cambridge, 1967.
2427 Sharf, Andrew. *The British press and Jews under Nazi rule.* 1964.
2428 Stansky, Peter and William Abrahams. *Journey to the frontier: Julian Bell & John Cornford: their lives and the 1930s.* 1966.
2429 Stephen, Barbara. *Girton College, 1869–1932.* 1933.
2430 Storey, Graham. *Reuter's century, 1851–1951.* 1951. History of the leading news agency.
2431 Tawney, Richard H. *The radical tradition: twelve essays on politics, education and culture,* ed. Rita Hinden. 1964.
2432 Thornton, Archibald P. *The imperial idea and its enemies.* 1959. 'Changes in attitude towards the British Empire . . . during the past hundred years.'
2433 Truscot, Bruce [Edgar Allison Peers]. *Red brick university.* 1943. Impressive for the interest it aroused.
2434 Tuke, Margaret J. *A history of Bedford College for Women 1849–1937.* 1939.
2435 Tylecote, Mabel. *The education of women at Manchester University, 1883 to 1933.* Manchester, 1941.
2436 Whates, Harry R.G. *The Birmingham Post, 1857: 1957.* Birmingham, 1957.
2437 White, Cynthia L. *Women's magazines 1693–1968.* 1970.
2438 Wiener, Martin J. *Between two worlds: the political thought of Graham Wallas.* Oxford, 1971.
2439 Williams, Bernard and Alan Montefiore (eds.). *British analytical philosophy.* 1966. By various authors.
2440 Williams, Raymond. *Culture and society 1780–1950.* 1958. And the con-

tinuation, *The long revolution*. 1961. 'A critical history of ideas and values.'

2441   Wood, Neal. *Communism and British intellectuals*. 1959.

4 Biographies
(See also sec. XI, pt. 4 and sec. XIII, pt. 4, above.)

2442   Barker, Nicolas. *Stanley Morison*. 1972. Morison was closely associated with a typographic revolution.

2443   Birkenhead, Frederick W.F. Smith, 2nd Earl of. *The Prof in two worlds: the official life of Professor F.A. Lindemann, Viscount Cherwell*. 1961.

2444   Braddon, Russell. *Roy Thomson of Fleet Street*. 1965.

2445   Brailsford, H.N. *The life-work of J.A. Hobson*. 1948.

2446   Carpenter, Luther P. *G.D.H. Cole: an intellectual biography*. Cambridge, 1973. And see (2449).

2447   Cecil, David. *Max, a biography*. 1964. Of Max Beerbohm.

2448   Clark, Ronald W. *The Huxleys*. 1968. On Julian and Aldous Huxley.

2449   Cole, Margaret. *The life of G.D.H. Cole*. 1971. See also (2446).

2450   Darlow, Thomas W. *William Robertson Nicoll, life and letters*. 1925. Biography of the editor of *The British Weekly, 1886–1923*.

2451   Ferris, Paul. *The house of Northcliffe. A biography of an empire*. New York, 1972.

2452   Forster, E.M. *Goldsworthy Lowes Dickinson*. 1934.

2453   Fyfe, Henry Hamilton. *T.P. O'Connor*. 1934. See also (418).

2454   Gardiner, Alfred G. *Life of George Cadbury*. 1923. Cadbury was a cocoa manufacturer, a newspaper proprietor and a social reformer.

2455   Grier, Lynda. *Achievement in education: the work of Michael Ernest Sadler, 1885–1935*. 1952.

2456   Hammond, John Lawrence Le Breton. *C.P. Scott of the 'Manchester Guardian'*. 1934.

2457   Harris, Henry Wilson. *J.A. Spender*. 1946. See also (2353).

2458   Havighurst, Alfred F. *Radical journalist: H.W. Massingham (1860–1924)*. 1974. See also (2338).

2459   Henderson, Archibald. *George Bernard Shaw: man of the century*. 1956. Detailed account of his political and social role as well as literary. For a closer examination of an important period, see Weintraub, Stanley. *Journey to Heartbreak: the crucible years of George Bernard Shaw, 1914–1918*. New York, 1971.

2460   Hobson, John A. and Morris Ginsberg. *L.T. Hobhouse: his life and work*. 1931.

2461   Hyman, Alan. *The rise and fall of Horatio Bottomley: the biography of a swindler*. 1972.

2462   Koss, Stephen E. *Fleet Street radical: A.G. Gardiner and the 'Daily News'*. 1973.

2463   Lekachman, Robert. *The age of Keynes*. New York, 1966. Largely biographical.

2464   MacKenzie, Norman and Jeanne MacKenzie. *H.G. Wells: a biography*. 1973. Latest and best.

2465   McLachlan, Donald. *In the chair: Barrington-Ward of 'The Times', 1927–1948*. 1971.

2466   Martin, Kingsley. *Harold Laski (1893–1950): a biographical memoir*. 1953. Re-established a leading figure in the intellectual world.

2467   Minney, Rubeigh J. *Viscount Southwood*. 1954. And the *Daily Herald*.

2468   Monroe, Elizabeth. *Philby of Arabia*. 1973. The life of an explorer, orientalist and author.

2469   Muggeridge, Kitty and Ruth Adam. *Beatrice Webb: a life, 1858–1943*. New York, 1968. Lively, popular, informed.

2470   Namier, Julia. *Lewis Namier, a biography*. 1971. Of a distinguished historian.

2471   Ogg, David. *Herbert Fisher, 1865–1940: a short biography*. 1947.

2472   Rolph, C.H. *Kingsley: The life, letters and diaries of Kingsley Martin*. 1973.

2473   Scott, Drusilla. *A.D. Lindsay: a biography*. Oxford, 1971. Lindsay was master of Balliol and then vice-chancellor of Oxford 1935—8.
2474   Strachey, Amy. *St Loe Strachey: his life and his paper*. 1930. Concerning the editor of *Spectator*, 1898—1925.
2475   Symons, Julian. *Horatio Bottomley: a biography*. 1955. See also (2461).
2476   Taylor, Henry Archibald. *Robert Donald*. [1934]. Donald was editor of the *Daily Chronicle*, 1902—18.
2477   Terrill, Ross. *R.H. Tawney and his times: socialism as fellowship*. Cambridge, Mass., 1973.
2478   Unwin, Philip. *The publishing Unwins*. 1972.
2479   Ward, Maisie. *Gilbert Keith Chesterton*. 1943. Biography of a significant poet, novelist and critic.
2480   West, Herbert Faulkner. *A modern conquistador: Robert Bontine Cunninghame Graham: his life and works*. 1932. Of a literary figure closely associated with political and social questions.
2481   Wood, Alan. *Bertrand Russell, the passionate sceptic*. 1957. A brief biography.
2482   Wood, Herbert George. *Terrot Reaveley Glover; a biography*. Cambridge, 1953. Glover was a noted classical scholar and historian.
2483   Wrench, John Evelyn. *Geoffrey Dawson and our Times*. 1955. Of the editor of *The Times*, 1912—19 and 1923—41.

5 Articles
(See also sec. XI, pt. 5 and sec. XIII, pt. 5, above.)

2484   Coppen, Helen (ed.). 'Symposium on mass media in the United Kingdom', *Year Book of Education 1960* (1960), 294—312. Inquiry from 1939 of use of mass media in education.
2485   Ferguson, John. 'The Open University in Britain', *World Year Book of Education 1972/3* (1972), 373—85.
2486   Freeden, Michael. 'J.A. Hobson as a New Liberal theorist: some aspects of his social thought until 1914', *JHI*, XXXIV (July—Sept. 1973), 421—43.
2487   Geyl, Pieter. 'Toynbee the prophet', *JHI*, XVI (no. 2, 1955), 260—74. Extended comment on Arnold Toynbee, *A study of history*. 1934—54, 10 vols.
2488   Himmelfarb, Gertrude. 'The intellectual in politics: the case of the Webbs', *JCH*, VI (no. 3, 1971), 3—11.
2489   Hopkin, Deian. 'Domestic censorship in the First World War', *JCH*, V (no. 4, 1970), 151—69.
2490   Hyde, William J. 'The Socialism of H.G. Wells in the early twentieth century', *JHI*, XVII (no. 2, 1956), 217—34.
2491   Irvine, William. 'Shaw, the Fabians, and the Utilitarians', *JHI*, VIII (no. 2, 1947), 218—31.
2492   Kitson Clark, G. 'A hundred years of the teaching of history at Cambridge, 1873—1973', *Hist. J.*, XVI (no. 3, 1973), 535—53.
2493   Lee, Alan J. 'Franklin Thomasson and the *Tribune*: a case study in the history of the Liberal press, 1906—1908', *Hist. J.*, XVI (no. 2, 1973), 341—60.
2494   Lockwood, John F. 'Haldane and education', *PA*, XXXV (Autumn 1957), 232—44.
2495   Mitchell, Harvey. 'Hobson revisited', *JHI*, XXVI (no. 3, 1965), 397—416.
2496   Mowat, Charles Loch. 'Social legislation in Britain and the United States in the early twentieth century: a problem in the history of ideas', in *Historical Studies*, (Papers read before the Irish Conference of Historians) VII (1969), 81—96.
2497   Peters, A.J. 'The changing idea of a technical education', *BJES*, XI (May 1963), 142—66.
2498   Pierson, Stanley. 'Ernest Belfort Bax: 1854—1926 — the encounter of Marxism and late Victorian culture', *JBS*, XII (Nov. 1972), 39—60.
2499   Samuels, Stuart. 'The Left Book Club', *JCH*, I (no. 2, 1966), 65—86.

2500   Soffer, Reba N. 'The revolution in English social thought, 1880–1914', *AHR*,
       LXXV (Dec. 1970), 1938–64.
2501   Szreter, R. 'History and the sociological perspective in educational studies',
       University of Birmingham Historical Journal, XII (1969–70), 1–19.
2502   Wiseman, Stephen. 'Higher degrees in education in British universities', *BJES*,
       II (Nov. 1953), 54–66.

INDEX OF AUTHORS, EDITORS, AND TRANSLATORS

Numbers are entry numbers except when otherwise specified